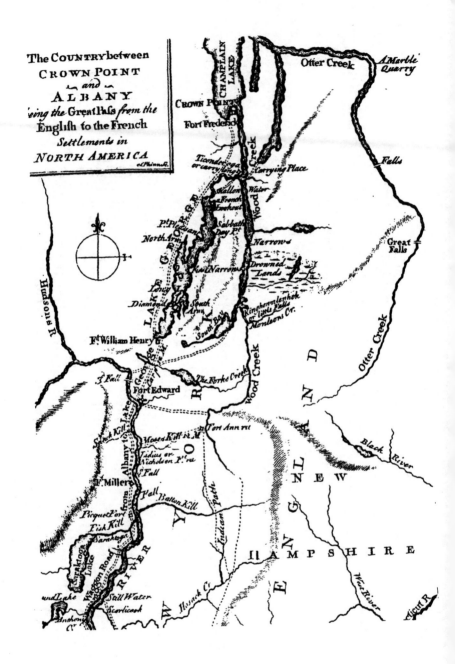

The COUNTRY between
CROWN POINT
and
ALBANY
being the Great Pass from the
English to the French
Settlements in
NORTH AMERICA

The French and Indian War
from
Scottish Sources

by
David Dobson

CLEARFIELD

Printed for
Clearfield Company, Inc. by
Genealogical Publishing Co., Inc.
Baltimore, Maryland
2003

International Standard Book Number: 0-8063-5211-6

Made in the United States of America

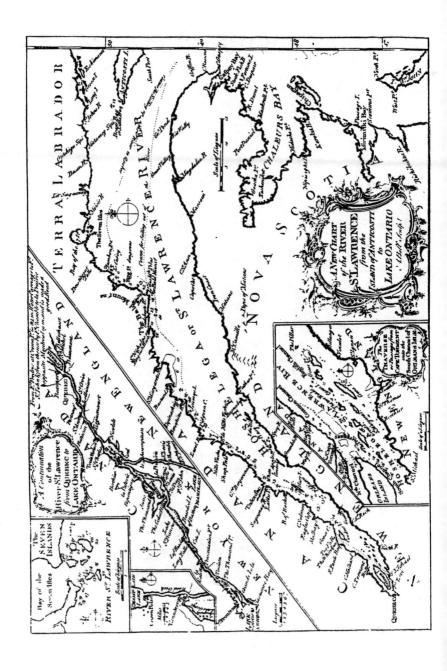

A NEW CHART of the RIVER S.T LAWRENCE from the ISLAND of ANTICOSTI to LAKE ONTARIO

A Continuation of the River S.T Lawrence from QUEBEC to LAKE ONTARIO

INTRODUCTION

During the mid-eighteenth century the power struggle between Great Britain and France erupted out of hostility and rivalry into open warfare. Known as the Seven Years War, it occurred between 1756 and 1763 and embraced warfare on three continents, Asia, Europe and America. In North America it is referred to as the French and Indian War. The eventual British success had major implications for the political structure of North America and the West Indies. Firstly, most of the former French colonies there became subject to Great Britain; and secondly, the elimination of the French presence in North America enabled the colonies to expand and become more self-reliant, which contributed to the movement towards independence. In the aftermath of the war there occurred a massive increase in emigration from the British Isles to the American colonies. Part of this was a direct result of the experiences gained by British soldiers who served there during the French and Indian War and either settled there immediately after the war or went home for their friends and families before returning. These soldiers not only defended the existing colonies but subsequently settled them. The British government, for their part, was keen to have experienced fighting men settled there who could defend the frontiers against Indian incursions. Many demobilised soldiers were granted land at strategic sites in areas such as the Mohawk Valley of New York.

But who were these men that made such a major contribution to the defense and later the settlement of colonial America? The records are far from complete and those that do exist are scattered throughout archives in Britain and North America. Some exist in military archives or museums, and others in private hands. There are many relevant documents in Scotland, especially in the National Archives of Scotland in Edinburgh, among the archival collections gifted or deposited there.

Although the oldest regiment of the British Army is the 1st Royal Regiment of Foot, usually known as the Royal Scots, it was not until the Seven Years War that Scottish regiments began to play a significant role in the British Army. During the war ten regiments were raised in the Highlands to fight both in Europe and America. The personal papers of many of their officers and men form the nucleus of this book.   That information is supplemented by data taken from a contemporary journal, the *Scots Magazine*, and a newspaper, the *Aberdeen Journal*. Places, events and people, not only Scots but English, Irish, French and Americans, are identified in this chronological compilation based solely on sources in Scotland.

Finally I should like to thank Lord Dalhousie for permission to quote from his family-papers.

David Dobson
St Andrews, Scotland
2003

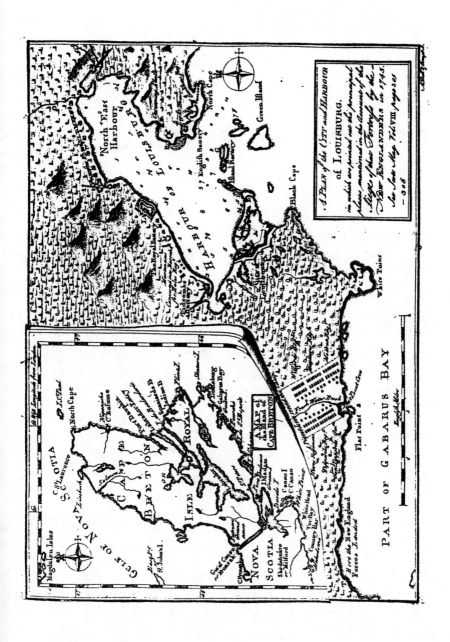

A PLAN of the CITY and HARBOUR of LOUISBURG.

PART OF GABARUS BAY

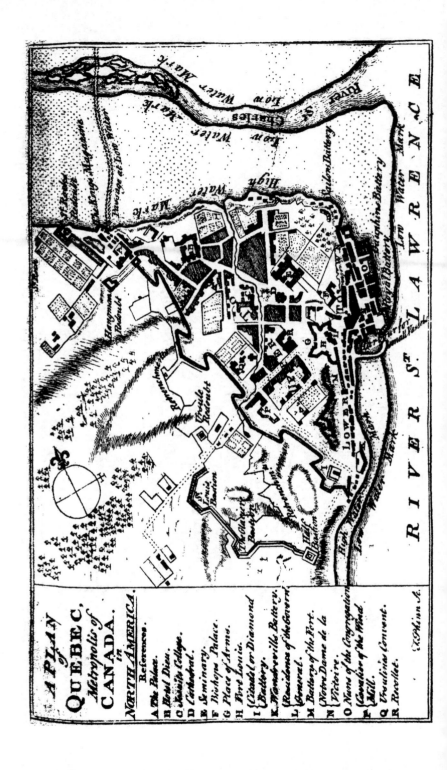

A PLAN of QUEBEC, Metropolis of CANADA, in NORTH AMERICA.

References.

A The Palace.
B Hotel Dieu.
C Jesuits College.
D Cathedral.
E Seminary.
F Bishops Palace.
G Place of Arms.
H Fort Louis.
I {Citadel or Diamond Battery.
K Heuvinville Battery.
L {Residence of the General. Corporal.
M Battery of the Fort.
N {Notre Dame de la Victoire.
O {Nuns of the Congregation. Convalescents of the Wood.
P Mill.
Q Ursuline Convent.
R Recollet.

KPhinn sc.

RIVER St. LAWRENCE

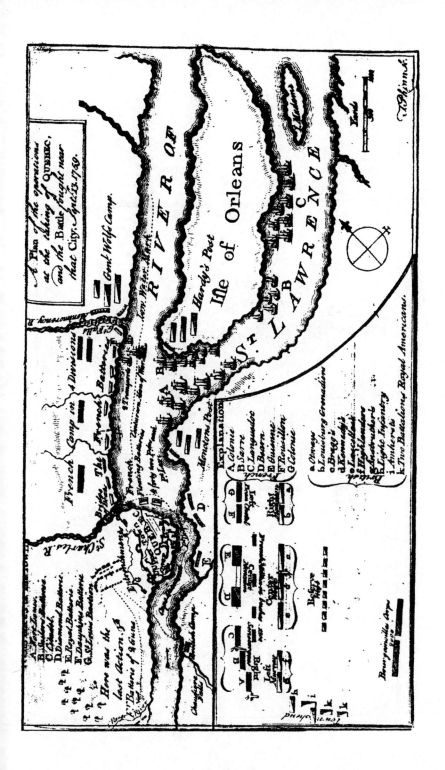

A Plan of the operations at the taking of QUEBEC, and the Battle fought near that City, April 13, 1759.

RIVER OF St LAWRENCE

Isle of Orleans

Hardy's Post

Genl Wolfe Camp

Montmorency R.

E. Fall

Ten Water Mark

The French Batteries

The French Camp on 4 Divisions

St Charles R.

French Camp

Homestone Post

A. Fortress
B. Lower
C. Upper Town
D. Richmond
E. Cap Rouge

Here was the last Action.

F.or Battery 9 Guns

Champlain

Explanation

French
A. Colonie
B. Sarre
C. Languedoc
D. Bearn
E. Guienne
F. Roussillon
G. Colonie

British
a. Otway
b. Louisburg Grenadiers
c. Bragg's
d. Kennedy's
e. Lascelles's
f. Highlanders
g. Anstruther's
h. Light Infantry
i. Amherst's
k. Two Battalions Royal Americans.

Phinn.

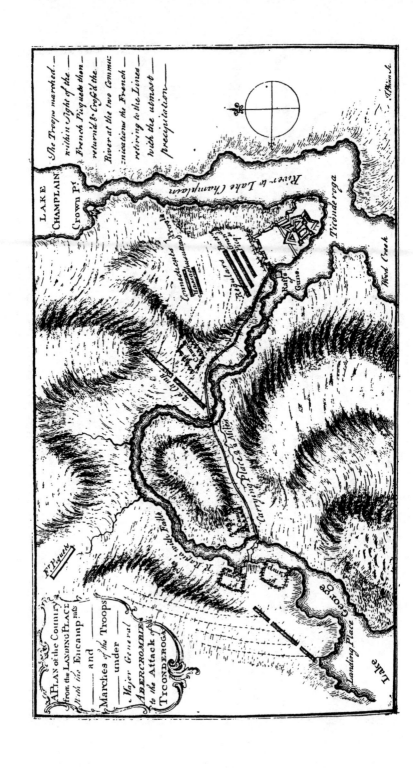

A PLAN of the Country from the LANDING PLACE With the Encampments and Marches of the Troops under Major General ABERCROMBIE to the Attack of TICONDEROGA

LAKE CHAMPLAIN

Crown P.t

The Troops marched within Sight of the French Piquets then return'd & Cross'd the River at the two Communications the French retiring to the Lines with the utmost precipitation

River to Lake Champlain

Ticonderoga

West Creek

The two Communications

Regular Bateaux

Ticonderoga

Fort of
Saw
Guns

Plain of 2 Miles

Carrying Place

Fort George

Landing Place

Fall of the
Bridge over the Falls

Ft.Pauch

Lake George

I.Penn &c.

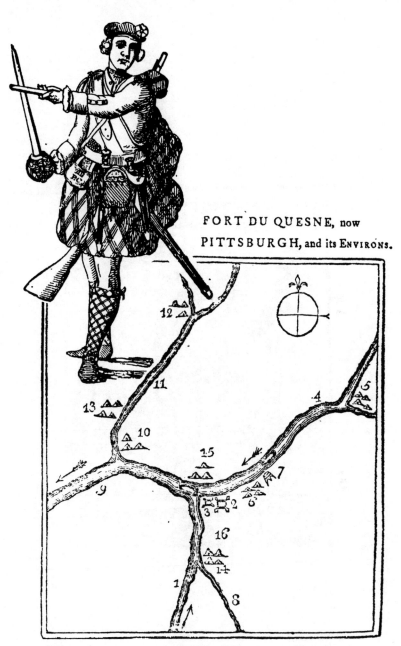

FORT DU QUESNE, now
PITTSBURGH, and its ENVIRONS.

1 *Monongahela river.*
2 *Fort du Quesne, now Pittsburgh.*
3 *The small fort.*
4 *Allegany river.*
5 *Allegany Indian town.*
6 *Shanapins.*
7 *The redoubt.*
8 *Yauyagany river.*
9 *Ohio or Allegany river.*
10 *Logs town.*
11 *Beavor creek.*
12 *Huskuskies, the chief town of the Six Nations.*
13 *Shingoes town.*
14 *Alleguippes.*
15 *Sennakaas.*
16 *Braddock's field.*

The arrows shew the course of the rivers.

THE FRENCH AND INDIAN WAR
FROM SCOTTISH SOURCES

SOURCE: NAS.NRAS#0631/35

A letter from James Leslie quoting a letter from Colonel Innes to Lord Fairfax with news of the reverse at Fort Duquesne in 1755.

****

SOURCE: NAS.NRAS#0631/35

Letters with news of General Braddock's death at Fort Duquesne, 1755

****

SOURCE: NAS.GD201.4.81

Letter regarding Clanranald's sons Donald, William and Normand joining Fraser's new Highland regiment, 27 January 1756.

****

SOURCE: NAS.GD105.396

Instructions to General Abercrombie on his appointment as Commander in Chief in North America, 1 April 1756.

****

SOURCE: NAS.NRAS#0631/35-40

Two letters from Lieutenant General Anstruther, concerning commissions in the Earl of Loudon's new regiment, the 60th Royal

American Regiment, and other requests for commissions under Loudon in America, 1755-1758

****

SOURCE: SM.18.237 [May, 1756]

17 May 1756, King George declared war on France.

****

SOURCE: Aberdeen Journal #435, [May 1756]

'At one o'clock came into town [ie Aberdeen] escorted by an officer's command of the Cameronian Regiment from Inverness, 34 impressed men from that county to join Lord Loudon's Regiment now destined for the American service'.

****

SOURCE: CA.III.422

'In May [1756] Lord John Murray's Regiment [the 42nd] was sent to America. Before sailing nearly 20 new officers were appointed, and 500 recruits joined the regiment. The following young Athollmen received commissions as Ensigns, on the Duke's recommendations – George McLagan, son of the Minister of Little Dunkeld, Patrick Balneavis, son of Edradour, and Patrick Stewart, brother to Bonskeid.'

****

SOURCE: SM.18.290, [June, 1756]

16 June 1756, King Louis declared war on Great Britain

****

SOURCE: SM.18.297 [June 1756]

HMS Lion, 40 guns, arrived in Boston on 4 April 1756 with £50,000 sterling, and HMS Woolwich, 500 tons, with 10,000 stand of arms and clothing aboard for the King's troops. On 18 March the French and Indians attacked 15 British battoes with provisions between Albany and Oswego and killed or took prisoners those on board. Mention of the French capturing a post near Oneida Falls twelve miles from Oswego where Colonel Mercer was in command. Reference to Colonel Broadstreet who had been unable to reach Oswego with a relief column.   General Shirley had left New York in early May bound for Albany. Sir William Johnson was to meet with various Indian chiefs at Onandago on 11 May where the river Indians of Ulster, Orange and Duchess counties were to be incorporated with the Mohawks, to secure the former against murdering any more British settlers. On 15 April the Governor of Pennsylvania declared the Delaware Indians to be traitors and rebels. British troops had been landed in Virginia, where in the Spring the Indian allies of the French had encroached up to 70 miles. Colonel Washington, with 70 men, had been besieged in Winchester by 5 or 600 Indians but was relieved by militia despatched by Governor Dinwiddie. On 15 April Notaway Indians and Cherokees had met with the Governor in Williamsburg and agreed to support the British.

****

SOURCE: Aberdeen Journal #453, [September 1756]

Extract of a letter from Boston dated 26 July regarding the French and Indian War, and a letter from the camp at Fort Hardy dated 18 July 1756.

****

SOURCE: SM.18.356 [July 1756]

A report that 14 Royal Navy ships were blockading Louisbourg but that several French men'o'war had arrived in Quebec with over 10,000 troops. Ships had arrived at New York with British troops including Highland regiments, and that 10,000 had been marched by General Winslow against Crown Point. 3,600 troops were sent to attack the French forts on Lake Ontario, including 300 sailors to navigate the vessels built there. General Johnson had gone to Onondago to negotiate with the Indians. The Indians on the Pennsylvania frontier had laid down the hatchet, whereas those on the Virginian frontiers had intensified their attacks. Colonel Washington had written to the Governor of Virginia who was sending the militia, also volunteers under Hon. Peyton Randolph. Funds were being raised to increase the line of forts along the frontiers of Pennsylvania and Maryland. Governor Glen of South Carolina had set out with an independent company of 60 men plus 50 provincials to build a fort in Cherokee country.

****

SOURCE: NAS.RH4/62

Letterbook, 1755-1756, of John, Earl of Loudoun, Commander in Chief in America,

****

SOURCE: NAS.GD24.1.840

Letters from Alexander Drummond to James Campbell, both lieutenants in Lord George Murray's 42nd Regiment of Highlanders, 1756.

****

SOURCE: NAS.RH4/77

Journal of John Grant, Lieutenant of the 42nd Highlanders, who served in the West Indies and North America during the Seven Years War 1756-1763. (microfilm)

****

SOURCE: NAS.NRAS#0631/38

Memorial and letter from the Master of Lovat regarding his intention to raise a regiment of Highland irregulars for service in America, 1756.

****

SOURCE: NAS.GD219.287.11

Letter on an expedition to build a fort among the Cherokees in South Carolina, 1756.

****

SOURCE: SM.18.399, [August 1756]

The Marquis de Montcalme, Governor in Chief in Canada, had arrived safely with his troops, and the Iroquois were opposed to the British. A report that Colonel Schuyler had beaten off an attack on Fort Ontario by 1000 French and Indians but had lost 26 men plus 6 regulars, and another involving Colonel Broadstreet in a skirmish near Oswego. 13 or 14,000 men had marched from Oswego to attack Crown Point. The Earl of Loudoun, arrived in New York on 26 July, and had set out for Albany to take command of the army. Reports from Charleston, SC, that the French and Indians had attacked the Chickasaw who the applied to South Carolina for assistance.

****

SOURCE: SM.18.459, [September 1756]

Sir William Johnson had persuaded over 200 Indians at the
conference at Onondago to join the British, and he had returned to
Fort Johnson on 7 July. General Winslow, the Commander of the
New England forces, had left Albany with 7000 Provincials bound for
Ticonderoga and Crown Point. A copy of the Articles between
Robert Dinwiddie of Virginia and the chiefs, sachems and warriors of
the Cherokees, subscribed by Peter Randolph, William Byrd, and 12
Cherokee leaders at Broad River, NC, on 17 March 1756.

****

SOURCE: SM.18.520, [October 1756]

Report that Oswego, after a 10 day siege, had been surrendered to
the French who had then burnt it. The French troops consisted of
three battalions of Sarre, Guyenne, and Bearn, plus colonists,
Canadians, and Indians under the Marquis de Vaudreuil. Colonel
Mercer, the commandant, had been killed and 1600 taken prisoner,
mainly from Shirley's and Pepperall's regulars plus part of Schuyler's
militia. Also Fort Granville on the Pennsylvania frontier had been
taken by French and Indians from Ohio.

****

SOURCE: SM.18.558, [November 1756]

Item discussing the reasons for the loss of Oswego including the
delay in reinforcing it with 850 men of the 44th Regiment then in
Schenectady. Copy of letter from Lord Loudoun to the Governor of
Rhode Island from Albany on 20 August. Reference to a Lieutenant
Kennedy who had married an Indian and become a tribal king.
General Abercrombie had allocated him a party of Highlanders who
accompanied the Indians on scalping expeditions. A letter from
Philadelphia dated 23 September stating that Colonel Armstrong of
Cumberland County had marched to fort Shirley on 30 August with
300 provincials, against Kittanning on the Ohio, 25 miles above Fort

Duquesne. On 3 September he reached Beaverdam, Frankstown, where Lieutenant Hog, and 12 men, was left to observe a group fo Indians, and next morning Armstrong attacked the Indians under Captain Jacobs, captured the town and released some prisoners. Mention of a skirmish between Catawba Indians and French Indians in North Carolina.

****

SOURCE: SM.18.616, [December 1756]

Letter from New England reporting that Eneas Bishop, a British captive who escaped from Canada, claimed that 13,000 French regulars and Indians had been sent to Crown Point to take the forts at Lake George then attack Albany. A report from Georgia that some Creek Indians had stolen horses from settlers on the Ogeachy but that the Creek elders had settled the matter before the situation worsened. Mr Pepper, the Indian agent of Georgia, was to have discussions with the Creeks.

****

SOURCE: NAS.CS16.1.99, p.116

Decreet in abstentia, John Innes of Leuchars, Captain in the Royal American Regiment, v. Elizabeth Gordon, 8 December 1756.

****

SOURCE: NAS.CS16.1.99, P131

Decreet in abstentia, Lieutenant Lauchlan Shaw of Captain Demeri's Independent Company in South Carolina, v. Captain Walter Stewart of General Ferrill's Regiment, 22 December 1756

****

SOURCE: NAS.NRAS.0029.

Letters from James Campbell at Camp Oswego concerning the war in America. 1755-1756.

****

SOURCE: NAS.NRAS#1275/96

Letters reporting on the war in America, particularly on Fort Du Quesne, Oswego and Crown Point, ca1756.

****

SOURCE: NAS.NRAS#1275/96

Letters from Ellis or John Huske to Charles Townsend with news from America concerning Fort Duquesne, the Siege of Oswego, Loudon at the Siege of Crown Point, and Sir William Johnson, circa 1756.

****

SOURCE: NAS.GD87.1.73/74

Commission to Alexander Campbell as Major in Lieutenant-Colonel Montgomery's 1st Highland Battalion of Foot, with a related letter from the Earl of Breadalbane, dated 7 January 1757 and 1 February 1757.

****

SOURCE: SM.19.55, [January 1757]

January 23, the King has been pleased to appoint the following gentlemen to be officers in two highland battalions of foot to be raised forthwith.

8

First Battalion. Lieutenant Colonel Commandant: Archibald
~~Montgomery, [brother to the Earl of Eglinton]; Majors: James~~ Grant,
Alexander Campbell; Captains: Hugh Mackenzie, John Sinclair, John
Gordon, Alexander Mackenzie, Roderick Mackenzie, William
McDonald, George Munro; Captain-Lieutenant, Alexander Macintosh;
Lieutenants: Alexander McDonald, James Grant, Robert Grant, Colin
Campbell, ...MacNab, Duncan Bayne, Joseph Grant, Nicholas
Sutherland, Hugh Gordon, Charles Farquharson, Cosmo MacMartin,
Donald Campbell, Alexander MacKenzie, Roderick MacKenzie,
James Duff, William MacKenzie, Alexander McDonald, ...MacDonald,
Henry Munro, Archibald Robertson; Ensigns: William Haggart,
Alexander Grant, Ronald MacKinnon, James Grant, William
MacLean, ...MacRah, Lewis Houston, ...McDoanld, George
Munro; Chaplain: Allan Stewart; Surgeon: Donald Stewart; Adjutant:
Alexander Montgomery.

Second Battalion. Lieutenant Colonel Commandant: Simon Fraser,
[eldest son of Simon late Lord Lovat]; Majors: James Clephane, John
Campbell; Captains: Thomas Fraser, John MacPherson, John
Campbell, Simon Fraser, Donald Macdonald, John Macdonnell,
Charles Baillie; Captain-Lieutenant, J. Crawford Walkinshaw;
Lieutenants: John Fraser, Archibald Macdonald, Simon Fraser,
Ronald McDonald, John MacDougal, Charles MacDonnell, Alexander
MacDonnell, Simon Fraser, William MacDonald, ...Mactosh, John
Murray, Rory MacNeil, Alexander Fraser, Archibald Campbell,
Donald McLean, James Fraser, Alexander McLeod; Ensigns: Simon
Fraser, Archibald Macallister, William Fraser, James Fraser, Allan
Stuart, Evan Cameron, Lachlan MacLachlan, ...Chisholm, John
Fraser; Chaplain: John MacLean.

****

SOURCE: NAS.RH4.77

Papers of John Grant, Lieutenant of the 42nd Regiment 1741-1763,
who fought in North America and the West Indies.

SOURCE: NAS.GD125.22.16.7

Papers of officers of the 63rd Foot, later the 78th, or Fraser's
Highlanders - Major James Clephane, 4 January 1757
Lieutenant Simon Fraser, brother to Dunballoch, 5 January 1757
Lieutenant Archibald MacDonald, brother to Clanranald, 18 January
1757.

****

SOURCE NAS.GD170/3431

Enlistment certificate in Lieutenant Colonel Montgomery's battalion of
John McPhail in Major Campbell of Barcaldine's company, 3 March
1757.

****

SOURCE: Aberdeen Journal #480, [March 1757]

A report of two battalions of Highlanders about to embark for
America.

****

SOURCE: NAS.GD125.22.16/17

Returns of recruits at Dundee for Major Clephane's company.

ALEXANDER BELL, 19 years, 5'3", enlisted in Dundee 10 February
1757, born in Kirriemuir, a laborer, fresh complexion, brown hair,
hazel eyes, round visage.

ALEXANDER FINDLAY, 17 years, 5'3", enlisted in Dundee 19
February 1757, born in Monifieth, a laborer, swarthy complexion,
black eyes, black hair, round visage.

PETER MOODY, 17 years, 5'1", enlisted in Dundee 20 February 1757, born in Glamis, a laborer, fresh complexion, black hair, hazel eyes, long visage.

WILLIAM MCKENZIE, 17 years, 5'2", enlisted in Dundee 20 February 1757, born in Kingoldrum, a weaver, fresh complexion, brown hair, grey eyes, long visage.

WILLIAM FIFE, 18 years, 5'2", enlisted in Dundee 21 February 1757, born in Kirriemuir, a weaver, fresh complexion, brown hair, hazel eyes, long visage.

GEORGE WRIGHT, 21 years, 5'5", enlisted in Forfar 24 February 1757, born in Brechin, a laborer, florid complexion, brown hair, hazel eyes, round visage.

DAVID MORRIS, 24 years, 5'3", enlisted in Perth 4 March 1757, born in Dron, a laborer, fresh complexion, brown hair, grey eyes, long visage.

PETER ROBB, 17 years, 5'3", enlisted in Careston 8 March 1757, born in Glamis, a laborer, fresh complexion, black hair, hazel eyes, long visage.

ANDREW LAIRD, 17 years, 5'3", enlisted in Dundee 10 March 1757, born in Cluny, Perthshire, a laborer, fresh complexion, brown hair, grey eyes, long visage.

JOHN MOLYSON, 18 years, 5'4", enlisted in Dundee 15 March 1757, born in the Mearns, a laborer, pale complexion, brown hair, grey eyes, long visage.

GEORGE GORDON,......, 5'2", enlisted in Dundee 17 March 1757, born in Kintore, a laborer, pale complexion, flaxen hair, ...

****

SOURCE: NAS.GD125.22.16.27

List of men to join Colonel Simon Fraser's Regiment.

David Munro	John Grant	Donald McKinnon
John Ross	John Sinclair	Hugh McKinnon
Norman Munro	Neill McNeill	John McDonald
Murdoch McLean.		

[1757?]

****

SOURCE: NAS.GD125.22.16.15

A Size Roll of Major Clephane's Recruits [1757?]
[probably recruited at Nairn for Fraser's Highlanders]

Thomas Kinloch	5'10"
Charles Rose	5'9.5"
Alexander Dunbar	5'8.5"
William Urquhart	5'8.5"
William Rose	5'8.5"
Alexander Rose	5'8"
Charles Falconer	5'8"
George Grant	5'8"
John Bremner	5'8"
Alexander Dunbar	5'8"
John Fraser	5'8"
Arthur Rose	5'7.5"
John McKenzie sr.	5'7.5"
Donald McKenzie	5'7"
David Rose	5'7"
John Fraser	5'7"
John McLeod	5'7"
Donald Ross	5'7"

FRENCH AND INDIAN WAR

Lachlan McIntosh	5'7"
James Kenneth	5'7"
John Anderson	5'7"
Matthew Miller	5'6.5"
Allan McDonald	5'6.5"
John McIntosh	5'6.5"
Rodrick McKenzie	5'6.5"
John McArthur	5'6.5"
Malcolm Ross	5'6"
James Tolmie	5'6"
John Ross	5'6"
Peter Smith	5'6"
Alexander Dunnoon	5'6"
Alexander McDonald	5'6"
William Sutherland	5'6"
George Sutherland	5'6"
Alexander Rose	5'6"
Thomas Russel	5'6"
John McKenzie	5'6"
Hugh Munro	5'6"
Finlay Fraser	5'6"
Alexander Smith	5'6"
Donald McIntosh	5'5.5"
John Robertson	5'5.5"
Hugh Munro	5'5.5"
William Chalmers	5'5.5"
James Russel	5'5.5"
John McIntosh	5'5"
Evan McBean	5'5"
Donald Ross	5'5"
Donald Bizet	5'5"
George Noble	5'5"
Donald McDonald	5'5"
John Ross	5'5"
Donald Cuthbert	5'5"
Rodrick Bain	5'5"
James Murray	5'5"

FRENCH AND INDIAN WAR

Alexander Bremner	5'5"
John Innes	5'5"
John Fraser	5'4.5"
Angus Stewart	5'4.5"
John Fraser	5'4.5"
John Cameron	5'4.5"
Donald McIntosh	5'4.5"
Hugh McCraw	5'4.5"
Niel McArthur	5'4.5"
Alexander Baxter	5'4.5"
Duncan Callam	5'4.5"
James Cuming	5'4"
Evan McDonald	5'4"
Duncan McCraw	5'4"
Murdoch McKenzie	5'4"
John Smith	5'4"
Charles Smith	5'4"
George McLeod	5'4"
Donald McDonald	5'4"
John Shearer	5'4"
Alexander McKenzie	5'4"
Donald Morison	5'4"
Donald Campbell	5'4"
James Fraser	5'4"
Finlay Munro	5'4"
Angus Munro	5'4"
James Fuller	5'4"
James Forbes	5'4"
William Falconer	5'3.5"
Alexander Fraser	5'3.5"
Andrew Ross	5'3.5"
James Fraser	5'3.5"
James Lamb	5'3.5"
James Noble	5'3.5"
Duncan Ross	5'3.5"
Edward Davidson	5'3.5"
Alexander Grant	5'3"

14

Murdoch Cameron	5'3"
Alexander McDonald	5'3"
Kenneth McPherson	5'3"
David Sutherland	5'3"
William Thomson	5'3"
William Ross	5'3"
Alexander McKenzie	5'3"
William Robertson	5'3"
Duncan Cameron	5'3"
Alexander Munro sr.	5'3"
Donald McPherson	5'3"
Alexander McKenzie	5'3"
Robert Graham	5'3"
Alexander Munro	5'3"
George Davidson	5'3"
John Grant	5'3"
John Keith	5'3"
David Cormack	5'3"
Grigor McGrigor	5'3"
Archibald Chisholm	5'2.5"
John Sutherland	5'2.5"
Alexander Stewart	5'2.5"
John Reid	5'2.5"
Donald Munro	5'2.5"
George Fraser	5'2"
James Bain	5'2"
Rodrick McLean	5'2"
Andrew Anderson	5'2"
Alexander Fraser	5'2"
George Urquhart	5'2"
John Sutherland	5'2"
Rodrick McKenzie	5'2"
John Cook	5'2"
John McKenzie	5'2"
David Ross	5'1.5"
John McDonald	5'6"
Alexander McArthur	5'7"

15

David McKenzie   5'4"
John Ross, volunteer
Alexander Rose, sergeant
John Watson, sergeant
James Gunn, drummer
James McDonald, drummer
Donald McGillvray, drummer
~~Alexander McLeod at~~ Nairn.

****

SOURCE: NAS.NRAS#0631/35-40

Letters from Lieutenant General Anstruther concerning commissions in the Earl of Loudoun's new regiment, the 60th {Royal American} Regiment; with other requests from commissions under Loudoun in America, 1755-1758.

****

SOURCE: SM.19.250, [May 1757]

Lord Loudon, before retiring to winter quarters, orderd two new forts to be built within a few miles of Lake George, one Fort Edward and the other Fort William Henry. On 19 January he arrived in Boston from New York to settle affairs there, and on 20 February he was due in Philadelphia to meet several colonial governors, where it was thought a plan to attack Cape Breton would be formulated. At the end of January Captains Rogers and Speakman with 70 men, captured 8 Frenchmen with provisions between Fort Edward and the French fort at Ticonderoga. The French send troops to release the 8 men but were driven off by the British. Captain Speakman and Lieutenant Kennedy and 16 others were killed, but Captain Rogers, though wounded, made it back to Fort Edward. A British squadron of 21 ships left Cork bound for North America on 8 May, along with 1000 soldiers of the 2nd Battalion of the Royal Scots, 700 of Forbes's, 700 of Blakeney's, 700 of Bragg's, 700 of Kennedy's, 700 of

Murray's, 700 of Perry's, 300 of 3 companies of the Train, and 700 of the Marines, under General Hopson, commander in chief, Lord Charles Hay, second in command, Colonels Perry and Forbes, Lieutenant Colonel Williamson, commander of the Train, Dugal Campbell, chief engineer, and 5 other engineers, in 55 transports.

****

SOURCE: NAS.NRAS#0631/39

Documents concerning Fort William Henry, Fort Edward, and the Otter Creek route to Lake Champlaine, 1756-1757.

****

SOURCE: NAS.GD170.3431

Enlistment certificate of John MacPhail in Major Campbell of Barcaldine's company of Lieutenant Colonel Montgomery's battalion, dated 3 March 1757.

****

SOURCE: NAS.NRAS#052/3

Commission by Commissary Joshua Loring for the construction of suitable boats to be made available at Lake George or Woods Creek, 1757.

****

SOURCE: SM.19.313, [June 1757]

A letter from Lancaster, Pennsylvania, dated 11 April claimed that 125 Catawba warriors were heading for Fort Cumberland, among whom was King Hagler who was seeking revenge for his son who had been killed last winter at Fort Duquesne, also that 3 or 400

Cherokees were to join the Catawbas. Letters from New York stated that there were 20,000 soldiers in Lord Loudon's army, encamped in the city and on Rhode Island. In mid-March a large body of French, Canadians and Indians unsuccessfully attacked Fort William Henry. Finally there were reports from America that a considerable number of French regulars had arrived at the Mississippi and in Hispaniola who were thought due to attack South Carolina.

****

SOURCE: SM.19.382, [July 1757]

Deaths, lately in North America, Captain George Douglas of Pepperall's Foot. He was eldest son of Captain David Douglas of Douglas's Foot, and grandson of Archibald Douglas of Cliftonhalls.

****

SOURCE: SM.19.375, [July 1757]

On 1st July the two Highland battalions, Montgomery's and Fraser's, sailed from Cork for North America.

****

SOURCE: SM.19.438. [August, 1757]

July, 1757. At Halifax, soon after his arrival, died Charles Perry Esq., Colonel of the 55th Regiment of Foot, lately raised in Scotland.

****

SOURCE: NAS.GD45.2.12.2

Return of the 2nd Battalion the Royal Regiment of Foot, commanded by Lieutenant General James St Clair, Halifax, 3 August 1757.

Anne and Mary
Lieutenant Colonel William Forster
Captain Robert Mirrie
Captain James Wall, of the Grenadiers
Lieutenant Henry Balfour
Lieutenant James Fenton
Lieutenant John Knox
Lieutenant Thomas Moncrieff
Lieutenant William Cook
Lieutenant Alexander Baillie
Ensign George Burton
10 sergeants
8 corporals
5 drummers
220 privates

Concord
Captain P. Gordon
Lieutenant William Cockburn
Lieutenant John Hill
Lieutenant John Gordon
Lieutenant Dudley Ashe
Ensign H. Waterson
Chaplain John Dick
Surgeon John McColme
9 sergeants
8 corporals
5 drummers
214 privates

Baltic Merchant
Captain Frederick Hamilton
Captain Alexander Hay
Lieutenant James Douglas, Quartermaster
Lieutenant James McManus
Lieutenant Frederick Newlands
Ensign Patrick West
5 sergeants
5 corporals
3 drummers

19

130 privates

Richmond Captain Benjamin Gordon
      Captain Robert Wilmot
      Lieutenant Archibald Hamilton
      Lieutenant James Stuart
      Ensign Robert Cook
      Ensign James Edington
      Surgeon's mate Arthur Burnside
      6 sergeants
      4 corporals
      4 drummers
      170 privates

Eagle Galley Lieutenant Charles Forbes
      Lieutenant Robert McKinnon
      Ensign Archibald Campbell
      Ensign Thomas Rothe
      Surgeon's mate John Cochrane
      6 sergeants
      7 corporals
      3 drummers
      150 privates.

****

SOURCE: SM.19.425, [August 1757]

The Earl of Loudon, with the transports from New York, arrived in Halifax, Nova Scotia, on 30 June, and Vice Admiral Holbourne, with the men'o'war and transports from Cork, arrived there on 9 July. The army in Nova Scotia is composed of 15 battalions, the Royal Scots, 2nd battalion, Forbes's, Whitmore's , Blakeney's, Bragg's, Hopson's, Lord John Murray's Highlanders, Kennedy's, Abercromby's, Warburton's, Lascelles's, Webb's, Perry's, and two battalions of the Royal Americans, besides 500 rangers, and 300 of the Royal Regiment of Artillery. The fleet has 19 ships of the line, 9 sloops and figates, 2 bomb ketches, and a fireship. Letters from New York say that Montcalm was advancing towards Albany with 9000 men whereas General Webb has only 4000 men there to oppose him. A letter from Fort William Henry dated 26 July says that Colonel John Parker, Captains Maginis and Ogden, plus lieutenant Campbell and Cotes of the New York Regiment and 350 men, went at night to attack the French at Ticonderoga but the plan misfired. Captains Maginis and Shaw, Lieutenants Campbell and Cotes, plus a captain of the New Jersey Regiment were killed, Captain Woodward was drowned, and Colonel Parker and Captain Ogden were wounded. Only 70 men returned alive – 280 were thought to be killed or taken prisoner, however 65 later returned. In Virginia there was concern about 2000 French and Indians on the road from Fort Duquesne to Fort Cumberland. Colonel Stanwix with 500 Royal Americans and provincials from Pennsylvania and Maryland had gone to oppose the French.

****

SOURCE: NAS.GD45.2.12.3

List of 17th Foot, commanded by Colonel John Forbes, on board the transports in Halifax harbor, 3 August 1757.

Constant Jane   Colonel John Forbes
                     Lieutenant Arthur Morrison

Major John Darby
Captain William Howard
Captain Lieutenant Rycalet
Ensign Williams
Lieutenant Colonel Morris
Ensign Martin
Lieutenant Tew
Ensign Robinson
Captain Howard
Lieutenant Duperron
11 sergeants

11 corporals
6 drummers
261 privates

Wellington

Major Derby
Captain Fowler
Lieutenant Hope
Ensign Harrison
Captain Edward Fowler
Captain John Vaughan
Ensign Montgomery
Earl of Dundonald
Lieutenant Caple St George
Lieutenant Lyon
7 sergeants
7 corporals
5 drummers
155 privates

Elizabeth

Captain Christopher Russell
Captain George Fullwood
Captain Russell
Lieutenant Walle
Ensign Savage
Lieutenant Gregory
Ensign Birchall
6 sergeants
6 corporals
4 drummers
133 privates

Blakeny

Captain Jocylyn White
Captain Vaughan
Lieutenant Roger, surgeon
Ensign Swetenham

22

Lieutenant Hughes
Robert Williams, Quartermaster
4 sergeants
5 corporals
3 drummers
108 privates

****

SOURCE: NAS.NRAS#0439/48-9

Journals of Lord Charles Hay who had served against the French in America, after his arrest in there awaiting court martial, 1758, and papers regarding the court martial, 1760.

****

SOURCE: NAS.NRAS#0631/441-444

Letter book of John, 4th Earl of Loudoun in America, referring to Oswego, Fort Ontario, the Indians, settlers, troops, etc, 1756-1758.

****

SOURCE: CA.III.430.

'By the Duke [of Atholl's] recommendation the three additional companies in the 42nd were given to – James Stewart of Urrard, James Murray, his Grace's nephew, and Thomas Stirling of Ardoch. Three of the new subaltern's belonged to Atholl, viz., Lieutenant Alexander Menzies, Ensigns Duncan Stewart, son of Derculich, and George Rattray, son of Dalralzion. The end of October the additional companies marched from Perth to Glasgow, where they remained till November 15th, when they marched to Greenock and embarked in transports for Cork en route for America.

Roll of Captain James Murray's Company, 42nd Highlanders, November 1757.

••

SERGEANTS: William Grant, Charles Robertson, John McQueen.
CORPORALS: John Leslie, Robert McLachlan.
DRUMMER: Alan Campbell.
PRIVATES: George Bremner, Donald Brown, Duncan Cameron, John Campbell, Donald Conacher, William Cowie, James Douglas, Donald Drummond, James Duncan, Alexander Fraser (1), Alexander Fraser (2), William Fife, Robert Grant, Alexander Irvine, James Kennedy, Duncan McAndrew, Donald McDiarmid, Archibald McDonald, (1), Archibald McDonald (2), Donald McDonald, John McDonald, William McDonald, Peter McFarlane, Alexander McIntosh, Robert McIntosh, William McIntosh, Donald McLean (1), Donald McLean (2), Thomas McNab, Alexander McPherson, James McPherson, Donald McRaw, Robert Menzies, William Munro, John Murray, Alexander Nicholson, Alexander Norrie, Alexander Reid, Alexander Robertson, Angus Robertson, Archibald Robertson, Charles Robertson, Donald Robertson, James Robertson (1), James Robertson (2), John Robertson, Peter Robertson, James Scroggie, Alexander Stewart (1), Alexander Stewart (2), Alexander Stewart (3), John Stewart, Robert Stewart, Thomas Stewart, William Stewart, John Wighton (1), and John Wighton (2).'

****

SOURCE: NAS.GD45.2.26.2

Letter from John Donaldson at Rogers, 8 October 1757.

****

SOURCE: SM.19.614, [November 1757]

October, 1757, died at Albany, Captain James Mercer of the 48th Regiment of Foot.

October 1757, died on passage from Halifax to New York, Major
General Dougal Campbell, Chief Engineer in North America.

****

SOURCE: SM.19.669, [December 1757]

September 1757, died at Albany, George Monro, Lieutenant Colonel
of Otway's Foot, in North America. He commanded at Fort William
Henry on Lake George when it was taken by the French.

****

SOURCE: NAS.NRAS#0631/39

Documents concerning Lord Charles Hay's service in America, 1757.

****

SOURCE: NAS.GD201.4.86

Letter from Roderick MacLeod with the news of the taking of Cape
Breton and that Donald is wounded, dated 24 August 1758.

****

SOURCE; SM.19.539.

 A report that Lord Loudon and Admiral Holbourne had held a council
of war at Halifax, Nova Scotia, on 4 August and on the basis of
reports indicating the strength of the French forces at Louisbourg and
of the French fleet there had abandoned any plan to attack them and
instead had left 3 battalions in Halifax and then returned to New
York. A letter from Fort Edward on Lake George stated that
Lieutenant Vanaght and a number of provincial soldiers under his
command had been killed and scalped, and from Albany came the
news that Indians had attacked Fort Edward on 23 July. Montcalm

aware that the majority of the British troops had gone to Halifax lay siege to Fort William Henry which was commanded by Colonels Monro and Young. 11,000 French troops and Indians surrounded 2500 British soldiers. On 9 August after a siege lasting a week Monro surrendered. The Articles of Capitulation appear as part of the report. The garrison was allowed to march from the fort escorted by French troops to within four miles of Fort Edward. However the column was attacked by the Indians with substantial casualties. On 21 July Colonel Parker of the New Jersey Regiment, with three of his companies, and two companies of the New York Regiment had left Fort William Henry on an excursion but were ambushed by the French heading for the fort. Of 350 soldiers, 150 escaped the rest being killed or taken prisoner.

****

SOURCE: NAS.GD45.2.25.1

Letter from Major Murray in Halifax reporting the loss of the Tilburn with all on board including Captain Croston, Lieutenant Dugdale and half a company of Grenadiers, 10 October 1757.

****

SOURCE: NAS.GD45.2.24.16

Recruiting instructions for officers of the 45th Foot commanded by Major General Warburton, signed by Major Murray of the 45th Foot, in Halifax 20 October 1757.

****

SOURCE: NAS.GD45.2.35.17.

List of men belonging to the regiment in Nova Scotia.

| John Walker | Daniel Stutley | 44th |

John Caton	William Sawl	48th
Richard Bush	Tall Rowlin	4 Battn.
James Clark		
John Malloy		
John Pikes	Lawrence Carter	1 Battn.

1757(?)

****

SOURCE: NAS.GD185.box 6, bundle 28.

Letter to Sir Robert Abercromby from Captain John Abercromby at Halifax on the capture of Fort William Henry by the French, French strength and dispositions in Canada, plus news of the garrison at Halifax, including reference to Captain Fesch of the Royal Americans whom General Montcalm took as hostage at the capitulation of Fort William Henry, 5 November 1757.

****

SOURCE: SM.19.599, [November 1757]

Accounts of the loss of Fort William Henry. On the morning of August 9 the garrison of Fort William Henry held a council of war, and having no help of a relief force arriving and as many of their guns were burst and there were only 17 shells left, the decision was taken to surrender. After agreeing terms of surrender Montcalm warned that the Indians anticipated plunder. Initially the Indians killed the sick and wounded then the Negroes, mullatoes and Indian soldiers, and finally they attacked the column bound for Fort Edward. Montcalm had been unable to control the Indians of 33 tribes under his command and in particular the Abenakis of Panaonanske in Acadia, especially once they had consumed rum looted from the British.

****

SOURCE: NAS.GD201.4.84

Letter from Roderick MacLeod on preparations for Fraser's Regiment, 63rd Foot, to sail to America, dated 24 November 1757.

****

SOURCE: NAS.GD45.2.24.3

A letter to Colonel John Forbes from John Cosnan, Captain of the 45th Foot in Boston, dated 28 November 1757, which refers to Ensign Wallis's recruit –

Henry Hammond, born in County Suffolk, New England, aged 18, 5'4", a laborer, enlisted in Boston 10 November 1757.

****

SOURCE: NAS.NRAS#0174

Letter from John Forbes stating that the army under his command was on its way to the Ohio River and Fort Du Quesne, that the Indian allies the Cherokees and the Catawbas had gone home, etc., [dated around 1757].

****

SOURCE: NAS.GD45.2.16

Plan and elevation of a blockhouse on the Hudson River near Fort Edward. [no date]

****

SOURCE: NAS.GD45.2.21

Letters from Lieutenant Colonel Arthur Morris of the 17th Foot, 1757-1758.

****

SOURCE: NAS.GD45.2.28

Letters from Lieutenant Colonel Haldimand of the 60th Foot, 1757-1758.

****

SOURCE NAS.NRAS#0333/1,5-9

Military papers of Brigadier General John Forbes, Sir John St Clair and General James Abercromby, 1755-1758

****

SOURCE. NLS#MS6506

Letters from Alexander and John Hamilton in Maryland to their brother Gavin Hamilton, a bookseller in Edinburgh, concerning the battle of Fort Du Quesne. [dated 1750s]

****

SOURCE: SM.20.51, [January, 1758]

November, 1757, died in America, Joseph Dusseaux, Colonel Commandant of the 3rd Battalion of the Royal American Regiment.

****

SOURCE: AJ #519

Extract from a letter from an officer of Montgomery's Highlanders in South Carolina dated 17 September 1757

****

SOURCE: NAS.GD25.22.17(18)

Weekly return of Captain John MacPherson's and Captain Donald McDonald's companies of Colonel Fraser's Highland Battalion at Millfort 12 December 1757.

Signed – John MacPherson

****

SOURCE: NAS.GD125.22.17(20A)

Return of Colonel Fraser's company at Stradford, 14 December 1757

1 Captain, 1 Lieutenant, 1 Ensign, 4 sergeants, 3 drummers, 104 men,
6 women victuallers

signed J. Fraser

Return of Captain Baillie's company of Grenadiers at Stradford 14 December 1757.

1 Captain, 2 Lieutenants, 4 sergeants, 2 drummers, 97 men, 7 women victuallers, Lieutenant Culbert's servant, Alexander McErtar musician.

Signed Captain Charles Baillie.

****

SOURCE: NAS.GD45.2.35/37

List of Officers of Hospitals in North America, 25 June to 24 December 1757

James Napier, Director
James Napier, Chief Surgeon
Dr Richard Huck, physician
John Adair, surgeon
George Munro, surgeon
William Russel, surgeon
William Young, surgeon
William Couce, apothecary
William Barr, apothecary
Simon Tiffen, apothecary
Jonathan Mullet, surgeon's mate
John Cochrane, surgeon's mate
William Austin, surgeon's mate
Robert Boyd, surgeon's mate
John Loch, surgeon's mate
Niel Lamart, surgeon's mate
Hugh Kennedy, surgeon's mate
John Charleston, surgeon's mate
John Waterhouse, surgeon's mate
William McMyne, surgeon's mate
Robert Bass, apothecary's mate
Francis Lucock, apothecary's mate
Joseph Williams, apothecary's mate
Donald Campbell, apothecary's mate
William Mitchell, apothecary's mate
William Baines, apothecary's mate
Richard Walker, apothecary's mate
James Ross, apothecary's mate
George Traill, apothecary's mate
John Wilson, apothecary's mate
Charlotte Brown, matron

****

SOURCE: NAS.GD45.2.33.1

Memorial by James Stevenson, ensign of the 50th Regiment, who had been appointed an Ensign in 1755, taken prisoner at the surrender of Oswego in August 1756, imprisoned in Canada until November when he was sent to France, exchanged in June and returned to America. Albany, 15 December 1757.

****

SOURCE: NAS.GD45.2.33.3

Memorial of James Campbell in the city of New York to Colonel John Forbes. James Campbell, son of Captain Laughlin Campbell who sailed from Islay in 1736 to New York where he conferred with Governor Cosby, now deceased, and Lieutenant Governor Clark and was granted several thousands of acres at Wood Creek on the route from Albany to Crown Point. In September 1738, August 1739 and November 1740 he brought over 500 loyal Protestants from Argyll to settle there but was unable to gain access to the grant, and then bought land in Orange County for his family. Captain Laughlin Campbell reurned to Scotland to fight the rebels in 1745 and died on his return to New York. James Campbell offers to serve as a Volunteer in Forbes's regiment. [no date]

****

SOURCE: NAS.GD248.49/1.

Letters from Francis Grant in Albany, New York, and Fort Edward, with occasional references to the campaign in America, 1756-1758.

****

SOURCE: NAS.GD45.2.41

Return of billets, 63rd Foot, Connecticut, January, 1758

****

SOURCE: NAS.GD125, box 34]

The orderly books of Fort Stanwix 1758-1759.

****

SOURCE: NAS.GD45.2.33.4

Memorial of Captain Thomas Jocelyn to John Forbes, Colonel of the 17th Regiment. He had become an Ensign of the 3rd Regiment in 1742, fought at the Battle of Dettingen, later he became a Lieutenant of the 3rd Regiment, he had come to America with General Braddock, he was a Captain at the taking of Oswego, and requests a recommendation to General Amherst. [no date]

****

SOURCE: NAS.GD45.2.29.2B

Proceedings of a Court of Inquiry held at Stratford, Connecticut, on 3 January 1758, by Lieutenant Colonel Simon Fraser of the 63rd or 2nd Highland Battalion concerning the manner of the death of Corporal James Mackay of the above regiment.

Members: Captain Charles Baillie, president; Lieutenant John Cuthbert, Lieutenant Charles McDonnell; Lieutenant John Fraser; and Ensign Simon Fraser'
Evidence given by William McHardy acting corporal refers to Sergeant Fraser, William McPherson a grenadier and Robert Robertson, soldier of the Colonel's Company. Also mentioned was Mrs Rudghers a brewer opposite Mr Buchanan's.

SOURCE: NAS.GD1.337.34.3

A letter from Robert Menzies of Culterallers containing news of friends wounded in America, 1758.

****

SOURCE: NAS.GD45.2.44

Letters and memos of Governor James Glen of South Carolina concerning Indian affairs and the state of forts, 1758.

****

SOURCE: NAS.GD45.2.51

Letters from Sir Allan Maclean of the 77th Foot, 1758.

■■

SOURCE: SM.20.220, [April 1758]

February 1758, died, at Piscataqua, Captain John Donckley, commander of the Enterprise, a man o'war.

****

SOURCE: NAS.GD45.2.22.7

Letter from Thomas Prather in Conoconeque to Sir John St Clair, deputy quartermaster, regarding provisions, 10 April 1758

****

SOURCE: NAS.GD45.2.22.8

Letter from James Wright to Sir John St Clair in Philadelphia regarding provisions, 15 April 1758.

****

SOURCE: SM.20.205, [April 1758]

Lord Loudon is recalled from America and command there is given to Major General James Abercrombie.

****

SOURCE: NAS.GD69.171

Letters from Arthur St Clair on service in North America, 1757/58

SOURCE: SM.20.245-249, [May 1758]

An account of the Expedition against Cape Breton.

****

SOURCE: NAS.GD18.4201/3/4

Letters from Mathew Clerk in New York regarding the war in America, 1757-1758. Letter from 'J.B.' vindicating the conduct of Mathew Clerk, chief engineer, at the Siege of Ticonderoga, 1758.

****

SOURCE: NAS.GD146, box 24/4

General orders by Major Jeffrey Amherst before the attack on Louisbourg, Cape Breton, 3 June 1758.

****

SOURCE: SM.20.316, [June 1758]

News from North America – two Highland battalions, with 9 additional
companies, and drafts from several regiments in Britain and Ireland
had arrived. There was by then a considerable body of regular
soldiers there, consisting of the 1st battalion of the Royal Scots,
Amherst's, Forbes's, Whitmore's, Blakeney's, Bragg's, Otway's,
Hopson's, Lord John Murray's highlanders, Abercromby's,
Warburton's, T. Murray's, Lascelles's, Webb's, Anstruther's, Howe's,
Royal Americans, four battalions, Montgomery's and Fraser's
Highlanders, drafts from Ireland, light infantry, and rangers, besides
artillery. Three expeditions were projected; one against Ticonderoga
and Crown Point, under the command of Major General James
Abercromby and Brigadier Lord Howe, at the head of 18,500 men,
consisting of the regiments of Blakeney, Murray's Highlanders,
Abercromby, Thomas Murray, Howe, Royal Americans, part of the 1st
and all the 4th battalion, Gage's Light Infantry, Roger's Rangers, and
the provincials of New York, New Jersey, Massachusetts Bay,
Connecticut, Rhode Island, and New Hampshire, plus 180 men of the
artillery; another against Fort Du Chesne under the command of
Brigadier Forbes, at the head of 6100 men consisting of part of the
1st battalion of the Royal Americans, Montgomery's Highlanders, the
provincials of Pennsylvania, Virginia and Maryland, and the
Cherokee Indians; and the third assault against Louisbourg, under
the command of Admiral Boscawen, Major General Amherst, and
Brigadiers Wolfe, Lawrence, and Whitmore, at the head of 12,900
regulars, consisting of the 1st battalion of the Royal Scots, Amherst's,
Forbes's, Whitmore's, Bragg's, Otway's, Hopson's, Warburton's,
Lascelles's, Webb's, Anstruther's, the 2nd and 3rd battalions of the
Royal Americans, Fraser's Highlanders, and drafts from Ireland,
provincials, etc. Letters from New York dated 30 May say that
General Abercromby was in Albany, and later marched to Fort
Edward on his way to Crown Point. Advice from Albany of March 20
indicate that Major Rogers had marched from Fort Edward on the

10th with 180 men, and on the 13th, five miles south of Ticonderoga, was attacked by 300 of the enemy, mostly Indians, and had to retire. A subsequent attack by the French and Indians caused the deaths of Captain Bulkely, Lieutenants Moore and Pottinger, Ensigns Ross, Macdaniel, Campbell and White, plus one volunteer, and about 137 taken prisoner. Only Major Rogers, Lieutenant Crofton and Ensign Waits had returned to Fort Edward. Letters from Albany dated 13 May claimed that 80 Indians and 4 Frenchmen attacked a British settlement at German Flats, near Fort Herchamer on April 30, killed 33 inhabitants but were driven off by a relief party of Rangers, of whom Lieutenant Hair was wounded.

****

SOURCE: AJ #549

Lists of troops engaged in the attacks on Louisbourg, Fort Du Chesne, Ticonderoga and Crown Point, including the Royal Scots, Fraser's Highlanders, Lord John Murray's 42nd Highlanders, and Colonel Montgomery's Highlanders, June 1758.

****

SOURCE: CA.III.437

Among the officers of the 42nd Regiment killed and wounded at Ticonderoga, the following were from Atholl –

ENSIGNS – killed, Patrick Stewart, brother to Bonskeid, and George Rattray, son of Dalralzion.
CAPTAINS – wounded, James Stewart of Urrard and James Murray, second son of Lord George Murray.
LIEUTENANT – wounded, Patrick Balneavis, son of Edradour.

****

SOURCE: NAS.GD87.1.82

Letter from Captain Allan Campbell of the 42nd Highlanders to his brfother John Campbell of Barcaldine, describing the defeat at Ticonderoga, listing Lts. John Campbell of Duneaves and Hugh McPherson as killed, and Major Duncan Campbell of Inverawe, his son Alexander, Captain John Campbell of Strathur, Lt. Archibald Campbell son of Archibald Campbell of Stonefield sheriff depute of Argyll, Lt. John Campbell of Glendaruel, Captain Graham of Muchray and his brother John, as wounded, dated 11 July 1758.

****

SOURCE: NAS.NRAS#0631/355

Letter from Lieutenant Colonel Bradstreet at Oswego regarding his landing near Cadaraqui 25 August 1758(?)

****

SOURCE: AJ #562

An extract of a letter from Winchester, Virginia, dated 6 August 1758 concerning troop movements and a proposed attack on the Ohio.

****

SOURCE: NAS.GD45.2.74

Memos on the North American campaign including a proposed campaign on the Ohio, 1758.

****

SOURCE: SM.20.430-439, [August 1758]

A detailed account of the Siege of Louisbourg.

State of the Garrison of Louisbourg, 26 July 1758, when it capitulated

24 Companies of marines of the usual garrison, and two of the artillery with 76 officers, 746 soldiers fit for duty, 195 sick and wounded, total 1017; 2nd battalion Volontaires Estrangers, 38 officers, 402 soldiers fit for duty, 86 sick and wounded, total 526; 2nd battalion Cambise, 38 officers, 466 soldiers fit for duty, 104 sick and wounded, total 606; 2nd battalion of Artois, 32 officers, 407 soldiers fit for duty, 27 sick and wounded, total 466; 2nd battalion of Bourgogne, 30 officers, 353 soldiers fit for duty, 31 sick and wounded, total 414; sea officers, men, marines, 135 officers, 1124 seamen fit for duty, 1347 sick and wounded, total 2606, grand total of prisoners 5637.

List of British troops killed and wounded

ROYALS. killed Lts. Fenton and Howe, wounded Lts. FitzSimmons, Baillie and Ashe; Ensign Waterson.
AMHERST'S. killed Lts. Nicholson and Campbell, wounded Lt Hamilton, Lt Adj. Mukins, Ensign Monypenny.
FORBES'S. killed Capt. The Earl of Dundonald, wounded Capt. Rycaut, Lt. Francis Tew.
WHITMORE'S. wounded Lts. Pierce Butler, John Jermyn, William Hamilton.
BRAGG'S. wounded Capt. Browne.
OTWAY'S. wounded Lts. Allan and Brown; Lt.Adj. Cockburn; Ensign Armstrong.
WEBB'S. killed Ensign Godfrey Rowe, wounded Lt. Hopkins.
ANSTRUTHER'S wounded Capt. Smith.
MONCKTON'S. killed Lt. Hart.
FRASER'S. killed Capt. Baillie; Lts. Cuthbert, Fraser and Murray; wounded Capt. Donald McDoanld; Lts. Alexander Campbell and John McDonald.
ROGER'S RANGERS. Killed Ens. Francis Carruthers
Killed 10 nco; 146 privates; wounded 7 nco, 2 drummers, 315 privates.

ARTILLERY . killed 1 gunner and 3 matrosses, wounded Col. Bastide the engineer in chief, 1 gunner, 3 matrosses. Total killed 172, wounded 353, 525 in all.

Report on the unsuccessful attack at Ticonderoga

Return of officers killed or wounded near Ticonderoga, 6 and 8 July 1758.

27th, LORD BLAKENEY'S Regiment, killed - Matthew Clerk, engineer; wounded Capts. Gordon, Holmes, Wrightson, Skene; Lt. Cook; Ensign Elliot.

42nd, LORD JOHN MURRAY'S Highlanders, killed – Capt.Lt. John Campbell, Lts. George Farquharson, Hugh MacPherson, William Baillie, John Sutherland; Ensigns Peter Stewart, George Rattray; wounded – Maj. Duncan Campbell; Capts. Gordon Graham, Thomas Graeme, John Campbell, James Stewart; Lts. William Grant, Robert Gray, John Campbell, James Grant, John Graham, Alexander Campbell, Alexander Macintosh, Archibald Campbell, David Mill, Patrick Balnevis; Ens. John Smith and Peter Grant.

44th, GENERAL ABERCROMBIE'S, killed – Ens. Fraser; wounded Maj. Eyre; Capts. Falconer, Lee, Bartman, Baillie; Lts. Treby, Simpson, Drummond, Pennington, Gamble, Dagworthy, and Greenfield.

46th, LT. GEN. THOMAS MURRAY'S – killed, Col. Beaver; Capts. Needham, Wynne; Lts. Laulke, Lloyd; Ens. Crafton; Ens.QM. Carfboncle; wounded Maj. Browning; Capts. Forbes, Marsh; Ens. Gordon.

55th, LORD HOWE'S – killed Brig.Gen.Lord Howe; Col. Donaldson, Maj. Proby; Capt.Lt. Murray; Lt. Stewart; wounded Capts. Bredin, Wilkins; Lt. LeHunt; Ens. Lloyd; QM French.

1st Battalion ROYAL AMERICANS – killed Capt.Lt. Forbes; Lt. Davis; wounded Maj. Tullikins; Capts. Munster, Mather, Cochran; Lts. Barnsley, Ridge, Wilson, Guy; Ens.Baillie, Gordon and Macintosh.

2nd Battalion ROYAL AMERICANS – killed Maj. Rutherford; Lt. Haselwood; wounded Capts. Prevost, Depheze; Capt.Lt. Slosser; Lt. Maclean, Allan, Turnbull, Macintosh.

LIGHT INFANTRY, COL. GAGE'S – killed Lt. Cumberford; wounded Capt. Gladwin; Ens. Paterson.

PROVINCIALS
COL. PREBBLE'S – wounded Capts. Winslow, Goodwin; Lts. Macomber, Dorman, Adam.
COL. DELANCEY'S – killed Lt.Adj.Muncey; Lt. Gatehouse; wounded Lt. Col. Leroux; Lts. Duncan, Degraw, Yates, Smith.
COL. BABCOCK'S – wounded Col. Babcock; Capt. John Whiting; Lt. Russell.
COL. FITCH'S – killed Lt. Howland; wounded Ens. Robins.
COL. BAGLEY'S – killed Lts. Burman, Low; wounded Capt.Whiple.
COL. JOHNSTON'S – killed Lt.Col.Shaw; wounded Capt.Douglas.
COL. WORSTER'S – wounded Lt.Col.Smedley
COL. PARTRIDGE'S – killed Capt. Johnson; Lt. Braggs; wounded Capt. A. Willard.

Extract from a letter from an officer at Lake George, 11 July.

Extract of a letter from a lieutenant in Howe's regiment at Lake George, 10 July.

****

SOURCE: SM.20.442, [August 1758]

July 6, killed in action near Ticonderoga, George Augustus Howe, Colonel of the 55th regiment

July 9, killed at the Siege of Louisbourg, William Cochran, Earl of Dundonald, a Captain in Forbes's Foot.

****

SOURCE: NAS.NRAS#0036, [Chalmers of Auldbar ms]

Letter from W. Skinner an army officer at Louisbourg on meeting with General Wolfe.

****

SOURCE: NAS.GD45/3/422-366

James Thompson, born 1732, to Canada with the Fraser Highlanders in 1758, later Overseer of Works in Quebec.

****

SOURCE: NAS.GD45.2.22.1/2

Letters from John St Clair at Croton Camp dated 24 September 1758 to Colonel Forbes

****

SOURCE: NAS.GD45.2.86

Letters of Colonel Henry Bouquet of the 60th Foot, 1758-1759

****

SOURCE: NAS.NRAS#0631/138

Letter from Abercrombie the engineer at Lake George 1758.

****

SOURCE: NAS.GD68.2.112

Letters from Dr Donald MacPherson at Halifax, Nova Scotia, 22 May 1758, and Mal MacPherson on his prospects with the army in New England.

****

SOURCE: SM.20.491, [September 1758]

A French account of the action at Ticonderoga.

****

SOURCE: NAS.GD45.2.22.3

Letter from John St Clair at Port Tobacco on the Potomac which refers to Captain Stewart of the Virginia Forces who was going to New York and Majors Robertson and Halket. [undated]

****

SOURCE: NAS.GD45.2.82

Papers of Captain Robert Stewart on raising a troop of horse rangers, 1758-1759.

****

SOURCE: NAS.GD45.2.33.2

A petition signed by the officers of a Virginia regiment asking for a Presbyterian chaplain. Subscribed in Carlisle Camp, 4 July 1758 by

Robert Bines	John Armstrong	David Kirkpatrick
James Piper	James Cuthbertson	Samuel Montgomery

FRENCH AND INDIAN WAR

Matthew Patton	Robert Robb	W. Hadden
Andrew Wilkins	William McDowell	John Jones
William Clinton	John Bryan	Hugh Cunningham
William M. Clay	David MacAlester	Daniel Boyd
Andrew Finlay	P. King	Robert Lattmore
John Hassel	Alexander McKean	John McClugham
Robert Boyd	Robert McPherson	John Byers
David Hunter	Thomas Hamilton	John McKnight
Richard Walker	John Montgomery	Charles McCling

****

SOURCE: NAS.GD45.2.3.16

List of deserters

Colonel Forbes'
John Winterbottom
Daniel Howard
Patrick McGinnis
Neal McMullen
Cornelius Haviland
James Lewis
George Penton

Colonel Whitmore's
John Standley
Thomas Franks
Roger Harvey
John Murray

Lord Blakeney's
Christopher Carson
John McGie
John Allan
John Buckley
Andrew McNeil
James Bell
John Hollam

Lawrence McKenzie
William McCarmick

Major General
Thomas Murray's   James Crawford
Thomas Buckley

Lieutenant Colonel
Perry's   Donald McDonald
John Criton

New York, 1758(?)

****

SOURCE: NAS.GD146.box24/4]

General orders by Major General Jeffrey Amherst before the attack on Louisbourg, 3 June 1758.

****

SOURCE: NAS.GD132.818

Commission to John Robertson as Lieutenant of the 42nd Foot commanded by Lord John Murray, 21 July 1758.

****

SOURCE: NAS.GD45.2.35.2

Return of the Corps which marched into Fort George, New York, 4 September 1757

17th Regiment
Colonel Forbes

FRENCH AND INDIAN WAR

Captain White
Ensign Paschal
Sergeant Norman Deane
Private Richard Whale
Private Richard Govey
Private John Downs
Private Daniel Sutton
Private Henry Lee
Private Peter Corney
Women Margaret Corney
      Elinor Whale
      Margaret Govey

22nd Regiment
General O'Farrel
Sergeant John Graham
Private Aaron Harrison
Private George Taylor
Private David Cree
Private Thomas Lockly
Private John Bartley
Private William Williams

27th Regiment
Lord Blakeney
Lieutenant William Jennick
Private Samuel Moore
Private Samuel Smith
Private Thomas Evans
Private Thomas Cotteral
Private Vincent Bayne
Private John Adams
42nd Lord George Murray
      Lieutenant Small
      Sergeant Colin McPherson
      Private Thomas Fraser
      Private Duncan Menzies

Private John Reid
Private William Fraser
Private Archibald McDermot
Private Fergus McGillvray
Women Elizabeth Fraser
Women Ann McOwen
Private Donald Smith
Private Alexander McOwen
Private Donald Symme
Private Alexander Stuart
Private Alexander Mill

44th Regiment
General Abercrombie
Corporal Samuel Swan
Private James Hellins
Private Tim Cotter
Private Alexander McDonald
Private James Wallace
Private William Anness
Private William Biggs
Woman Jane Anness

46th Regiment
General Thomas Murray
Sergeant Matthew Slinger
Private John Bevan
Private James Smith
Private Samuel Burgall
Private Patrick McGough
Private Patrick French
Woman Mary French
Woman Elizabeth McGough

48th Regiment
Corporal John Ashworth
Private David White

Private Francis Thompson
Private Patrick Mulvanney
Private William Armstrong
Private John Satchel
Private Martin Mooney

55th Lt. Col. Berry's
Sergeant Donald McDonald
Private John Campbell
Private Robert Kinneir
Private William Tosh
Private John Murray
Private David Richards
Private Thomas Jordan
Woman Elizabeth McDonald
Woman Jane Murray

60th, 2nd Battalion the Royal Americans
Lord Loudoun
William Deally
John Handyman
James McMullen
William Lloyd
Richard Edwards
Josh Steel
Woman Ann Steel
Woman Mary McMullen

****

SOURCE: NAS.GD45.2.35.3

Return of men listed in America, discharged and to be dismissed in New York. Albany, 24 September 1757.

Christopher Colstead of Major Fletcher's company
Abraham McCoy of Captain Collin's company

****

SOURCE: NAS.GD45.2.35.4

Return of men enlisted in Europe and return of proposed men
discharged and not recommended. Albany, 24 September
1757.

Robert Schouphollam in General Olway's company
Richard Yexley in Colonel Munro's company
John Slaughter in Major Fletcher's company
William Newberry in Major Fletcher's company
Daniel O'Bryan in Captain Maunsell's company
John Fryer in Captain Maunsell's company
Edward Powell in Captain Collin's company
John Hodge in Captain Collin's company
William Lewis in Captain Fletcher's company
Robert Jones in Captain Fletcher's company
Thomas Fletcher in Captain Bellew's company
William Higgins in Captain Bellew's company
James Halls in Captain Bellew's company
Richard Robinson in Captain Bellew's company
Joshua Taylor in Captain Bellew's company
John Williams in Captain Ormsby's company
William Martingall in Captain Ormsby's company
John Parey in Captain Ince's company

****

SOURCE: NAS.GD45.1.35.5

Report of Fort George guard, New York, 14 October 1757, deserters
courtmartialled.

	Regiment	Company
Disney Lynch	2nd Battalion,	Captain

	Royal Americans	Broadstreet
Rowland Brown	Independent Company	Captain Cruickshank
James McLeod	Colonel Berry's	Captain Monipenny
William Richards	Independent Company	Captain Cruickshank
Christopher Carr	Independent Company	Captain Cruickshank
John Ward	Independent Company	Captain Cruickshank
Richard Lutwyche	General Webb's	Captain French

****

SOURCE: NAS.GD45.2.24.4b

Weekly return of recruits raised by Captain Cosnan of the 45th Regiment of Foot, commanded by Major General Hugh Warburton, Boston 2 January 1758.

Name description	Trade	Size	born	enlisted	age	
John Holland	tailor	5'6"	Ireland	Boston	15	straight Wellmade
Wm.Fitzgerald	laborer	5'7"	Ireland	Boston	21	dark Complexion Dark eyes Brownhair

SOURCE: NAS.GD45.2.35.7

Weekly return of the recruits of the 40th Regiment, commanded by Major General Hapson, week ending 15 January 1758.

John Bergabine, born in Germany, 5'9", a husbandman, enlisted in Boston 11 January 1758. Description, complection yellow, hazel eyes, and black hair.

****

SOURCE: NAS.GD45.2.35.6

Return of the 35th Regiment's unfit, Philadelphia 9 January 1758.
■■

John Holmes	35 years service
James Houghton	1 year 8 months service
Richard Marlow	1 year 8 months service
William Beaumon	4 years service
John Warrington	1 years service
Charles Hilliard	1 years service
John Connolly	1 years service
Patrick O'Neill	1 years service
Isaac Sim	7 years service
Richard Bentin	1 year 8 months service
William McNeil	1 years service
John Hogan	1 year 8 months service
Richard Gregory	1 year 8 months service

Signed Henry Fletcher, Major 35th Regt.

****

51

SOURCE: NAS.GD45.2.87

Correspondence of Colonel Archibald Montgomery of the 77th Foot, 1758-1759.

****

SOURCE: NAS.GD45.2.35.10

Weekly return of Recruits of the 47th Regiment commanded by General Lefodis, Boston, week ending 16 January 1758.

Enos Bartholemew, born in Windham, 37, 5'7", a farmer, enlisted in Boston. Description: dark complection, well made

Peter Brewer, born on Long Island, 20, 5'8", a cooper, enlisted in Boston. Description: fair face and sandy hair

Joseph Grant, born in Salem, 5'8", a shoemaker, enlisted in Boston. Description: well made and a fresh color.

George Everson, born on the Island of Jersey, 26, 5'7", enlisted in Boston. Description: light brown with a long visage.

****

SOURCE: NAS.GD45.2.35.9

Weekly return of Recruits for the 40th Regiment by Ensign John Archbold, in Boston 10 January 1758.

Richard Dun, born in Ireland, 18, 5'5", a laborer. Description: ruddy complection, grey eyes and brown hair.

Patrick Healy, born in Ireland, 17, 5'4", a laborer. Description: brown complection, strong made, black eyes and black hair.

Edward Correy, born in Ireland, 18, 5'6", a joiner. Description: stong made, grey eyes and brown hair.

****

SOURCE: NAS.GD45.2.24.5

Letter from John Cosnan to Colonel Forbes –

"the recruits picked up here are generally Irish such as have been at the fishing season at Newfoundland so may judge they are not such as will mend a regiment that has been so long abroad as ours – however we are glad to get any that have the appearance of service in them."

Boston, 18 January 1758.

****

SOURCE: NAS: GD45.2.35.11

Return of Engineers in North America

Captain Lieutenant William Green, at Albany
Captain Lieutenant William Eyre, with his regiment
Captain Lieutenant George Weston, at Fort Edward
Captain Lieutenant Harry Gordon, in Philadelphia on leave
Captain Lieutenant Adam Williams, at Albany
Captain Lieutenant Matthew Clark, at Albany.

Subscribed in New York 31 January 1758.

****

SOURCE: NAS.GD45.2.35.13

Discharge papers of Thomas Baily, late of His Majesty's 22nd Foot, Captain Robert Wrey's company, served 15 years, at New York 15 April 1758.

****

SOURCE: NAS.GD45.2.36.3

Return of recruits in New England by the Nova Scotia officers.

Royals	Lieutenant McKinnon	1
	Lieutenant Moncrieff	10
	Lieutenant Cook	6
40th	Captain Mackay 13	
	Lieutenant Cottnam	6
	Ensign Archbold	24
45th	Captain Cosnam 3	
	Ensign Wallace	8
47th	Captain Cox 4	
	Ensign West	2
	Ensign Nicholson	2

New York, 6 February 1758.

****

SOURCE: NAS.GD45.2.83.3/RH1.2.509

Return of the Virginia Regiment commanded by George Washington at Fort Loudoun, 1 March 1758.

FRENCH AND INDIAN WAR

Companies	Place
Colonel Washington	Winchester
Major Lewis	Jackson River
Captain Waggener	South Branch
Captain Stewart	Winchester
Captain McNeill	Jackson River
Captain Lewis	Patterson Fort
Captain Woodward	Roanoke
Captain McKenzie	South Branch
……….	Winchester

30 commissioned officers
4 staff officer
30 sergeants
15 drummers
675 rank and file
125 short.

This excludes 2 companies ordered to Carolina.

Subscribed George Washington.

****

SOURCE: NAS.GD45.2.35.12

Return of the Brigade of Engineers in New York.

William Green	at Albany, ordered to Halifax
William Eyre	at Albany, with the 44th
George Weston	at New York, ordered to Halifax
Harry Gordon	at Fort Edward, ordered to Halifax

Adam Williams   at Albany

Matthew Clerk   at Albany, ordered to Halifax

John Williams   at Fort Edward

John Montresson   in the Jerseys

> J. Montresson, Lieutenant Colonel,
> New York, 17 March 1758.

****

SOURCE: NAS.GD45.2.35.19

Return of the Invalids of 3 Battalion

Drum Major Templeton
                    Hays
                    Baperman
                    Walgrove
          John Allan
                    Butcher
                    Fallonfield
                    Rice
                    Brownfield
                    Fowler
                    Joieux
                    Roxhead
                    Sherridan
                    McDermitt
                    McDonnall
          John Brown
                    Lamb
                    Knox
                    Porter

Willson
Sergeant Gubbin
Sergeant Smith
Speide
Andrew Bower
Neal
Will McIntosh
Cornet Hanly
Sherlock
Names
Broom
Logan
Hobbard
Hars
Mahoney
Spence
Tucker

Subscribed by J. W. McKenzie, surgeon, 1758(?)

****

SOURCE: NAS.GD45.2.35.13

Discharge certificate of Thomas Baily, private of the 22nd Foot, in Captain Wrey's company for 5 years, transferred to Brigadier General Forbes' regiment.

Subscribed T. Rollo, Colonel
New York, 15 April 1758.

****

SOURCE: NAS.GD45.2,22.6

Letter from John Wright in York County to Sir John St Clair, dated 16 April 1758.

****

SOURCE: NAS. GD45.2.36.5

Return of 4 company, 1st Battalion, the Royal American Regiment, commander Major General Abercrombie.

Brigadier General Stanwix, with 3 commisioned officers, 3 staff officers, 6 non-commissioned officers, and 99 men.

Captain Herbert Munster, with 3 commissioned officers, 6 non-commissioned officers, and 96 men.

Captain Richard Mather, with 2 commissioned officers, 6 non-commissioned officers, and 100 men.

Captain Gavin Cochrane, with 2 commissioned officers, 6 non-commissioned officers, and 99 men.

Captain William Stewart, with 2 commissioned officers, 6 non-commissioned officers, and 99 men.

Subscribed John Tulliken, Major, at Phiadelphia 22 April 1758.

****

SOURCE: NAS.GD45.2.36.6

Return of the 2nd Virginia Regiment, commanded by Colonel William Byrd, 12 June 1758.

Colonel William Byrd, with 4 commissioned officers, 5 staff officers, 5 non-commissioned officers, and 80 men.

Major William Peachey, with 3 commissioned officers, 6 non-commissioned officers, and 80 men.

Hancock Eustace, with commissioned officers, 6 non-commisioned officers, and 78 men.

John Fields, with 3 commissioned officers, 4 non-commissioned officers, and 95 men.

John Lighfoot, with 2 commissioned officers, 4 non-commissioned officers, and 82 men.

John Posy, with 3 commissioned officers, 5 non-commissioned officers, and 96 men.

Thomas Hemings, with 1 commissioned officer, 5 non-commissioned officers, and 82 men.

John Rootes, with 3 commissioned officers, 5 non-commissioned officers, and 79 men.

Samuel Meredith, with 3 commissioned officers, 5 non-commissioned officers, and 80 men.

****

SOURCE: NAS.GD68.Sec.2, 112.

Letter from Malcolm MacPherson at Halifax giving news of the prospects of the army in New England, 22 May 1758.

****

SOURCE: NAS.GD45.2.22.5

Letter referring to the Earl of Loudoun, the Maryland Forces, Dr Ross, and Fort Cumberland, dated 3 June 1758 at McDarnall's near Fredericktown

****

SOURCE: NAS. GD45.2.36.6

Weekly return of the 2nd Virginia Regiment, commanded by Hon. William Byrd, 12 June 1758

Colonel William Byrd
Major William Peachey
Thomas Cocke
Hancock Eustace
John Fields
John Lightfoot
John Posey
Thomas Fleming
John Rootes
Samuel Meredith

****

SOURCE: NAS.GD87/82

A letter from Allan Campbell, Captain of the 42nd Highlanders to his brother John Campbell of Barcaldine informing him of the defeat at Ticonderoga on 8 July 1758 and listing Lieutenant John Campbell of Duneaves and Lieutenant Hugh McPherson as killed, and Major Duncan Campbell of Inverawe, his son Alexander, Captain John Campbell of Strathur, Lieutenant Archibald Campbell son of Archibald Campbell of Stonefield sheriff depute of Argyll, Lieutenant John Campbell of Glendaruel, Captain Graham of Muchray and his brother John as wounded. Lake George, 11 July 1758.

****

SOURCE: SM.20.698

A letter written by an officer of Lord John Murray's Regiment at Fort Edward on 17 August 1758 reporting on the action at Ticonderoga.

****

SOURCE SM.20.547, [October 1758]

A report concerning the western expedition against Fort Du Quesne, under the command of Brigadier Forbes. Including an extract from an officer, dated at Fort Loudon, 17 July 1758 which mentions Ray's town on the road between Littleton and Carlisle, where a strong fort was being built, Indians under Colonel Bouquet scouting near Fort Du Quesne, troops include 350 Royal Americans, 1200 Highlanders, 2600 Virginians, 2700 Pennsylvanians, and 1000 wagoners, settlers, etc. An extract from a letter from New York regarding the expedition against Fort Du Quesne. A letter from Philadelphia dated 28 September 1758 reporting on military action near Fort Du Quesne – Major Grant with 838 men had marched from Lyal Henning and attacked the fort but had been driven off – among those missing in action were – Royal Americans, Lts. Billings and Ryder, Ensigns Rohr and Jenkins, and 35 privates; Highlanders, Major Grant, Capts. Munro, Hugh Mackenzie, Macdonald, Lts. A. Mackenzie, Colin Campbell, W. Mackenzie, Roderick Mackenzie, Macdonald jr., Ensign John Macdonald, 131 privates; Virginians, Major Lewis, Lts. Baker and Campbell, Ensigns Allen, Chew and Guest, 61 privates; North Carolinians, 4 privates; Marylanders, Lt. McCrea and 22 privates; Pennsylvanians, Ensign Haller and 18 privates; Lower Counties, 2 privates; total missing 295, returned 543. A report from Louisbourg that it now being taken specified regiments were left to garrison it and the rest returned to New York. St John's Island had been captured by the Royal Americans under Lord Rollo.

****

SOURCE: AJ #567

Report on the aftermath of the Siege of Louisbourg.

****

SOURCE: AJ #572

Extract of a letter from Virginia concerning the Siege of Fort Du Chesne, 14 September 1758.

****

SOURCE: CA.III.440

Roll of Captain John Reid's company of the 42nd Regiment, commanded by Captain James Murray during the expedition in New York in October 1758.

Captain James Murray, wounded
Lieutenants Kenneth Tolmie, and David Mill, wounded
Ensign Charles Menzies
Sergeants, James McNab, John McAndrew, John Watson and Alexander Cumming
Corporals, John Cumming, Jonathan Grant, Angus McDonald and John Stewart
Drummers, Walter McIntyre killed, and Alan Campbell
Privates, William Anderson, John Buchanan killed, Angus Cameron, Hugh Cameron killed, William Carmichael, Donald Carr killed, Hugh Christie, Alexander Cumming, James Farquharson killed, Alexander Fraser, Donald Fraser (1), Donald Fraser (2), Hugh Fraser (1), Hugh Fraser (2), John Forbes, John Graham, Donald Grant, James Grant, John Grant (1), John Grant (2), William Grant, James Gordon, William Gordon, Donald Kennedy (1), Donald Kennedy (2), John Kennedy, George McAdam, John McArthur, Donald McColl, Donald McDiarmid, Angus McDonald, Archibald McDonald (1), Archibald McDonald killed, James McDonald killed, John McDonald, Lachlan McDonald, William McDonald killed, Neil McEachern, Peter McFarlane killed, John McGillivray, Leonard McGlashan, Alexander McGregor, Donald McGregor, Robert McGregor, John McIntosh, Alexander McIntyre, Donald McIntyre, James McIntyre killed, Hector McInven, Hugh McKay, Alexander McKenzie, Hugh McKenzie, John McKenzie (1) killed, John McKenzie (2), Roderick McKenzie, Dougall

McLachlan killed, John McLaren, Roderick McLean, Neil McLeod, Norman McLeod killed, Donald McLeish (1), Donald McLeish (2), William McLinnion, Neil McMillan, Donald McNeil killed, Neil McNeil, Hugh McPhee, John McPhee, Alexander McPherson, Donald McQueen killed, James Michall, Donald Murray, James Murray, James Rea, Alexander Reid, Alexander Ross, Donald Ross, Hugh Ross killed, John Ross, Donald Robertson, Neil Shaw, John Sinclair died of wounds, John Smith, Walter Spalding, Alexander Stewart, Charles Stewart died of wounds, Donald Stewart died of wounds, Walter Stewart died of wounds, Robert Urquhart, Donald Watson, Donald Wheet, William Wishart, and Duncan Wright.

****

SOURCE: NAS.GD45.2.35.14

Report of the Guard at Lowell Hannon, 6 November 1758.

Subscribed by John Dagworthy, Lieutenant Colonel, Maryland Forces.

John McDonald and John Kendall of the Virginians returned from Captain Woodrow's detachment. Major Jamieson came in with a party of 150 men. Two suttling wagons belonging to Mrs Smith came in. Samuel Stellmaker's guides came in with 2 wagons belonging to Colonels Montgomerie and Byrd. Captain Sinclair of the Highlanders came in with a detachment. Mr Bisset ensign arrived. A wagon belonging to Mr Basset came in. Samson White of Colonel Byrd's battalion returned from captain Woodrow's. Fifteen of the Volunteers belonging to Maryland left the camp with discharges from Captain Shelby. Charles Boyle of Captain Thomson's Light Horse came in with letters to Sir John Sinclair. Mr Sinclair, Deputy Quartermaster Hooper and Mr Clark the commissary and Lieutenant Bryan, with a party of 15 men came in.

****

SOURCE: SM.20.659, [December 1758]

Advice from America. The French had launched an attack on 12 October on Brigadier Forbes advance guard at Loyal Hanning on the road to Fort Du Quesne but had been repulsed. A letter from Fort Cumberland dated 17 October says that the enemy numbered 1200 French and 200 Indians. Lt. James Duncanson of the Virginians was wounded; Lts. Pratter and Mathew of the Marylanders were killed, and Ensign Bell wounded; also wounded was Lt. Wright of the artillery. The action near Fort Du Quesne was reported in the Maryland Gazette of 8 October and provided a list of the wounded – Royal Americans, Capt. Lauder, Lt. Bentinck, 70 privates; Highlanders, Lts. Archibald Robertson, Henry Monro, Macdonald sr., Ensign Alexander Grant, Surgeons Dunnet and Harris, 162 privates; Virginians, Capts. Bullet and Walter Stew, 104 privates; Carolinians, 7 privates; Marylanders, Capts. Ware, and Riley, Ensign Harrison, 50 privates; Pennsylvanians, Capt. Clayton, Lts. Hays, Reynolds, 8 privates.

****

SOURCE: NAS.GD45.2.22.4

Letter from John St Clair referring to Mr Faquier, Captain Posey, and to the 2 Virginia Regiments and the 3rd Pennsylvania Regiment, dated 7 December 1758 at Ray's Town.

****

SOURCE: NAS.NRAS#0859/70

Letter from John Douglas at Fort Stanwix, 1758.

****

SOURCE: NAS.GD87/84

A letter to John Campbell of Barcaldine from Captain Allan Campbell giving news of Lieutenant George Campbell in General Gage's Regiment (a son of Barbaldine) and of Major Alexander Campbell (another son of Barcaldine) at Fort Du Quesne and of the death of Major Duncan Campbell of Inverawe, after the retreat from Ticonderoga. New York, 1 January 1759.

****

SOURCE: AJ #585

Extract of a letter from Pittsburgh [formerly Fort Du Chesne] dated 2 January 1759 to a gentleman in Aberdeen stating that General Forbes had appointed Captain Alexander McKenzie of Balmoir, of Montgomery's Highlanders, as Governor of the Fort.

****

SOURCE: NAS.GD45.2.35.15

List of Commissions {no date}

60th Regiment

Lieutenants:	Robert Stewart Archibald Blane Edward Jenkins
Ensigns:	Francis Pfister .....McDougall William Leslye
Quartermaster:	Lieutenant James Dow

64th Regiment {Montgomerie's}

Captain	Alexander McIntosh	Charles Farquhar

FRENCH AND INDIAN WAR

Captain Lieutenant   Nicholas Sutherland

Lieutenant	Alexander Grant	William Haggart
	Louis Houston	William McLean
	James Grant	John McDonald
	Raynold McKinnon	

Ensign	Allan Stuart	John Dunnet
	James Grant	Alexander Menzies
	John McKenzie	Alexander Grant
	Alexander Munn	

****

SOURCE: NAS.GD185.

State of executry account of Captain James Abercromby of the Royal Regiment of Foot, who died at Louisbourg in 1758, 1759.

****

SOURCE: NAS.GD18.4201/4804/4205

Letters re Matthew Clerk, son of Sir John and Lady Mary Clerk, chief engineer at the Siege of Ticonderoga, dated 1757-1759.

****

SOURCE: NAS.GD77.200.6

Letter on the expedition to Guadaloupe, dated 18 April 1759.

****

SOURCE: NAS.GD224.box 297/bundle 6

A letter from David Wooster at Lake George giving details of his service since 1741, dated 1759.

****

SOURCE: NAS.GD170/3432

Enlistment certificate in Robert Murray Keith's Regiment of Duncan McNicol in Captain Patrick Campbell's Company, 20 October 1759

****

SOURCE: NAS.GD224, box297/bundle 6

A letter from James Wall at Stillwater to Townsend at Saratoga concerning the garrison at Stillwater, 1759.

****

SOURCE: NAS.GD45.2.36.7

Effective return of the Pennsylvania Regiment
at Carlisle 25 December 1758.

Officers and their posting

Lieutenant Humphries	Pittsburg
Ensign Falkner	Pittsburg
Lieutenant Colonel Lloyd	Legonier
Captain Weiser	Legonier
Lieutenant Miles	Legonier
Lieutenant Clapham	Legonier
Ensign Handler	Legonier
Ensign Morgan	Legonier

Ensign Quicksell	Stoney Creek
Captain Clayton	Fort Bedford
Lieutenant Attlee	Fort Bedford
Lieutenant Scott	Fort Bedford
Lieutenant McKie	Fort Bedford
Lieutenant Patterson	Fort Littleton
Ensign Graden	Fort Littleton

Companies

Colonel James Burd	38 rank and file
Colonel Lloyd	44 rank and file
Major Shippen	37 rank and file
Lieutenant Colonel Work	34 rank and file
Major Jameson	33 rank and file
Major Ornds	44 rank and file
Captain Busee	46 rank and file
Captain Hambight	35 rank and file
Captain Morgan	29 rank and file
Captain Trump	11 rank and file
Captain Weiser	45 rank and file
Captain Clayton	33 rank and file

At Pittsburg -	2 sergeants
At Legonier –	7 sergeants, 2 drummers
At Stony Creek -	1 sergeant, 1 drummer
At Bedford -	6 sergeants, 3 drummers
At Littleton -	2 sergeants, 3 drummers

****

SOURCE: NAS.GD45.2.33.5.

Memorial to Brigadier General John Forbes by James Milne, surgeon's mate of the 1st Battalion of the Royal American Regiment, who had come from Scotland with Lord Loudoun. Subscribed Carlisle, 6 January 1759.

****

SOURCE: SM.21.272, [May 1759]

February 27, died in Guadaloupe of a flux, Major General Peregrine Thomas Hopson, Colonel of the 40th Regiment of Foot, and Commander in Chief of the Forces employed in the West India Expedition.

March 11, died in Philadelphia, aged 40, John Forbes, son of the deceased Colonel John Forbes of Pittencrieff, Fife, a Brigadier General, Colonel of the17th Regiment of Foot, and Commander of the British troops in the southern provinces of North America. His corpse was interred in the chancel of Christ's Church in Philadelphia.

****

SOURCE: NAS.GD45, sect.2/97

Brigadier General John Forbes, probate 24 March 1759
Pennsylvania

****

SOURCE: NAS.GD45.2.33.6

Memorial to General Forbes from Samuel Nelson, late Captain of a company in the service of Pennsylvania. Subscribed in Philadelphia, 1759.

****

SOURCE: NAS.GD45.2.1-105

Letters and papers of Brigadier General John Forbes.

****

SOURCE: NAS.GD45.2.36.8

Return of the Maryland forces at Fort Cumberland under Captain Richard Pearis 8 January 1759.

4 officers, 5 non commissioned officers, and 61 rank and file

****

SOURCE: NAS.GD45.section 2/97

Copy of the will of Brigadier General John Forbes, probate 24 March 1759, Pennsylvania.

****

SOURCE: NAS.GD45.2.36.14

List of officers and regiments (no dates)

Captain Hay	Royal
Lieutenant Hamilton	General Amherst's
Captain Holmes	Lieutenant Blakeney's
Lieutenant Gore	General Otway's
Ensign French	General Otway's
Captain Harvey	General Abercrombie's
Lieutenant Francis	General Abercrombie's
Lieutenant Downes	General Murray's
Ensign Ewan	General Lascelles'

Captain Mather	Royal Americans
Captain Cumberbatch	Royal Americans
Captain Gladwyn	Light Infantry
Captain Ogilvy	Independent Company
Lieutenant Lee	General Warburton's
Lieutenant Webb	General Webb's
Lieutenant Maxwell	General Amherst's

****

SOURCE: NAS. GD45.2.38.4

Return of 17th Foot commanded by Colonel John Forbes at Fort Edwards.

Colonel John Forbes
Lieutenant Colonel Arthur Morris
Major John Darby
Captain Christopher Russell
Captain Edward Forster
Captain Jocelyn White
Captain John Vaughan
Captain William Howard
Captain George Fullwood
William, Earl of Dundonald

23 commissioned officers
4 staff officers
26 non-commissioned officers
687 rank

subscribed Arthur Morris, Lieutenant Colonel.

****

SOURCE: NAS.GD21/674

Commission by John Blair, President of HM Council and Commander in Chief of the colony of Virginia in favor of John Peebles as a surgeon's mate in the 2nd Virginia Regiment, 1 June 1758.

****

SOURCE: SM.21.312, [June 1759]

A proclamation by the Governor of Nova Scotia concerning land grants there.

****

SOURCE: NAS.GD87/85

Letter to John Campbell of Barcaldine from his son Major Alexander Campbell giving news of friends serving in America. Fort Edward, 19 June 1759.

****

SOURCE: NAS.CS16.1.105, p.78

Decreet, James McPherson, late merchant in Glasgow, now a Lieutenant in the Highland Regiment commanded by Colonel Montgomery in America, 26 June 1759.

****

SOURCE: NAS.RH15.38.145

Letters from William Scrogie, late servant to Brigadier General John Forbes, giving value of possessions in General Forbes' house in Pennsylvania, June 1759.

****

SOURCE: NAS.RH15.38.81, 83

Memorial re the services of Brigadier General Forbes in his
expedition to the Ohio and Fort Du Quesne, 1758/1759.

****

SOURCE: NAS.GD87/87

A letter from Major Alexander Campbell to his father John Campbell
of Barcaldine informing him that the French had abandoned the fort
at Ticonderoga on 26 July 1759. Ticonderoga, 27 July 1759.

****

SOURCE: NAS.GD.248.507/3

Letter from Captain Robert Grant at Ticonderoga, referring to capture
of the fort there, 1759.

****

SOURCE: NAS.GD170/1067

Letter from Allan Campbell on the capture of Fort Ticonderoga and
the hope of taking Crown Point, 27 July 1759.

****

SOURCE: NAS.GD298.404

Letter from Lieutenant Hugh Gordon describing the attack at
Ticonderoga and its abandonment by the French, 27 July 1759.

SOURCE: SM.21.386, [July 1759]

Died in New England, Brigadier General Waldo, 'well known for his zeal in raising a regiment and going with it against Louisbourg in the last war.'

****

SOURCE: NAS.CS16.1.104

Decreet, Mrs Margaret Laurie v. Walter Kennedy presently in the British service in America, eldest son of William Kennedy in Leffanhill, 11 July 1759

****

SOURCE: NAS.CS16.1.105

Decreet, in abstentia. David Monro, Writer to the Signet, V. Lt. Donald McBean of Colonel Fraser's Highlanders, 25 July 1759.

****

SOURCE: NAS.CS16.1.105, P.256

Reference to Captain Archibald Campbell of the Royal Highlanders, 4 August 1759.

****

SOURCE: NAS.GD87/88

A letter from Major Alexander Campbell to his father John Campbell of Barcaldine with news that his regiment under General Amherst had taken Crown Point and that a detachment under General Prideaux had taken Niagara. Crown Point, 6 August 1759.

****

SOURCE: NAS.GD21/675

Commission by Archibald Montgomery, Colonel of the 1st Highland Battalion, in favor of John Peebles as surgeon's mate, 15 August 1759.

****

SOURCE: NAS.CS16.1.105, p.218

Act etc, Hugh Fraser of Laidclune v. Donald Hossack soldier in Colonel Fraser's Highlanders, 11 August 1759.

****

SOURCE: SM.21.439, [August, 1759]

A letter from Major General Jeffrey Amherst, dated Crown Point 5 August 1759, to Mr William Pitt in Whitehall, reporting on the action between 27 July and 5 August around Ticonderoga and Crown Point. Reference to Brigadier General Prideaux, Brigadier General Gage, Lieutenant Moncrieff, Sir William Johnson, and Lieutenant Colonel Eyre. Copy of a letter from Sir William Johnson to Major General Amherst, dated Niagara 25 July, advising him that Niagara had surrendered to the British that day.

****

SOURCE: SM.21.444, [August 1759]

Died, in Guadaloupe, Colonel Cunningham, chief engineer in the expedition against that island, 1759.

Died on 6 July 1759, in New England, aged 63, Lieutenant General Sir William Pepperell

****

SOURCE: NAS.NRAS#0631/374

Letter concerning the return of Amherst to Crown Point after the unsuccessful campaign at Lake Champlain, 1759.

****

SOURCE: SM.21.487, [September, 1759]

A letter from James de Lancey, Lieutenant Governor of New York to Mr William Pitt, dated New York 5 August 1759. A letter from Lieutenant Coventry to Lieutenant Governor de Lancey, dated Albany 2 August 1759, giving an account of the taking of Niagara. A list of ordnance and stores captured at Niagara, signed by George Wray, clerk of stores. A letter from a captain of the Royal Highland Regiment dated Fort Edward 6 August 1759 giving details of the British operations in North America.

****

SOURCE. SM.21.501, [September, 1759]

Died in July from a cannon shot from Fort Ticonderoga, Colonel Roger Townsend, youngest brother of George and Charles Townsend.

****

SOURCE: NAS.GD170/3432

Enlistment certificate of Duncan McNicol in Captain Patrick Campbell's Company of Robert Murray Keith's Regiment, 20 October 1759.

****

SOURCE: NAS.GD202.68.12

Report of the Siege of Quebec and death of Dungallon there, 1759.

****

SOURCE: AJ #615

Item concerning the surrender of Quebec on 18 September 1759 including lists of killed or wounded officers of Fraser's Highlanders.

****

SOURCE: AJ #616

A letter from an officer of Colonel Fraser's Regiment dated Quebec 20 September 1759 listing officers killed and wounded.

****

SOURCE: NAS.GD216#188/213

Commission to Sir James Cockburn as an Ensign in Lord John Murray's Regiment of Foot in North America, 1746; with Wolfe at Quebec 1759.

****

SOURCE: AJ #623

Captain Simon Fraser of Colonel Fraser's Regiment, second son of Charles Fraser of Inverallochy, died in Quebec on 15 October 1759 of wounds received on 13 October 1759.

****

SOURCE: SM.21.541, [October 1759]

A letter from Major General Wolfe and Vice Admiral Saunders to at Montmorency on the St Laurence to William Pitt dated 2 September 1759, with an attached list of the killed, wounded and missing -

AMHERST'S – killed surgeon's mate, 2 sergeants, 9 privates; wounded Major Irving, Captain Loftus, Lt. Rutherford, Lt, Adj. Mukins, Lt Leslie, Enss. Worth and Barker, 4 sergeants, 1 drummer, 45 privates.
BRAGG'S – killed 1 sergeant, 13 privates, wounded – Capt. Mitchelson, 1 sergeant, 1 drummer, 54 privates, missing – 2 privates.
OTWAY'S – killed Capt. Fletcher, Lt. Hamilton, 1 sergeant, 22 privates, wounded – Capt. Ince, Lts. Gore, Blakeney and Field, 1 sergeant, 1 drummer, 38 privates.
KENNEDY'S – killed 9 privates, wounded – Capt. Maitland, Lt. Clements, 13 privates, missing 1 private.
LASCELLES's – killed Lt. Matthison, 2 sergeants, 14 privates, wounded – Capt. Smelt, Lts. Elphinston and Mountain, 2 sergeants, 1 drummer, 44 privates.
WEBB'S – killed Lt. Percival, 13 privates, wounded Col. Burton, Capt. Edmiston, Lt. Adj. Hathorn, Lt. QM Webb, 2 sergeants, 45 privates, missing 2 privates.
ANSTRUTHER'S – killed 9 privates, wounded Capt. Leland, Lt. Hayes, Lt QM Grant, 2 sergeants, 1 drummer, 42 privates.
MONCKTON'S – killed Capt. Ochterlony, Lts. Kennedy and de Witt, Ens. Johnson,17 privates, wounded Capt. Lt. Brigstock, Lts. Escuyer, Granider, Archibold, and Howarth, Ens.Peyton, 4 sergeants, 89 privates, missing 1 sergeant, 4 privates.

LAURENCE'S – killed 1 sergeant, 1 private, wounded Major Prevost, 3 sergeants, 23 privates.
FRASER'S – killed 18 privates, wounded Col. Fraser, Capts. MacPherson and Simon Fraser, Lts. Cameron, McDonald and H. McDonald, 1 drummer, 85 privates, missing – 2 privates.
GRENADIERS OF LOUISBOURG – 1 sergeant, 9 privates, wounded Capt. Hamilton, Lts. Collingwood, Bradstreet and Jones, 2 sergeants, 1 drummer, 62 privates.
 Wounded – Capt. Bell, adc to the commander in chief
ENGINEERS – wounded, Capts. Williamson and Green.
RANGERS – killed Capt.Lt. Armstrong, Lt. Meech, 1 sergeant, 20 privates, wounded – Capt. Danks, Lt. Stephens, 4 sergeants, 24 privates, missing – 1 private.
ARTILLERY – 4 privates
MARINES – killed 8 privates, wounded 2 privates.

A letter from Charles Saunders on the <u>Stirling Castle</u>, off Point Levi, on the River St Lawrence, 5 September 1759.

A letter from General Robert Monckton, dated 15 September 1759, Point Levi Camp on the River St Lawrence, to William Pitt.

A letter from Brigadier General Townsend, dated 20 September 1759 in camp before Quebec, including the terms of capitulation, lists of arms found in Quebec 18 September, and lists of the killed, wounded or missing dated 13 September 1759 –

General Staff Officers, killed Maj. Gen. James Wolfe, wounded Brig. Gen. Monckton, Col. Carleton the QM General, Capt. Spittal major of brigade, Capt. Smyth, ADC, Maj. Barre the adj, general.
AMHERST'S – killed 2 privates, wounded Lt. John Maxwell sr and John Maxwell jr, William Skeen, Robert Ross, 5 sergeants, 52 privates.
BRAGG'S – killed - Lt William Cooper, 1 sergeant, 3 privates, wounded – Capts. Ralph Corry, Acomb Millbank, Thomas Spann, Lts. William Evans, ... Buxton, Ens. William Henry Fairfax, 4 sergeants, 1 drummer, 28 privates.

OTWAY'S – killed, Lt. William Mason, 6 privates, wounded, Capts. Charles Gore, Richard Allen, Gabriel Maturin, James Cockburn, 1 sergeant, 28 privates

KENNEDY'S: killed 3 privates, wounded, Ensign Jones, 2 sergeants, 18 privates

LASCELLES – killed, Lt Seymour, 1 private, wounded Capt. Gardiner, Lts. Peach, Gwynnett, Ewer, Henning, Ensigns Dunlop, Faunce, 1 sergeant, 2 drummers, 26 privates

WEBB'S – wounded, 3 privates

ANSTRUTHER'S – killed, Ens. Tottenham, 8 privates, wounded, Capts. Nuttall, Bird, Lts. Kemptie, Grant, Ens. Dainty, 80 privates

MONCKTON'S – killed 5 privates, wounded Capt.Sam. Holland, Lts. James Calder, James Jeffrey, Alexander Shaw, Ensigns Charles Cameron, William Snow Steel, 2 sergeants, 1 drummer, 80 privates, missing 1 private

LAWRENCE'S – wounded, 2 privates

FRASER'S – killed, Capt. Ross, Lts. Rory McNeil, Alexander McDonnell, 1 sergeant, 14 privates, wounded, Capt. John McDonnell, Simon Fraser, Lts. Ronald McDonnell, Archibald Campbell, John Douglas, Alexander Fraser sr., Ensigns James McKenzie, Alexander Gregorson, Malcolm Fraser sr., 7 sergeants, 131 privates, missing 2 privates

Louisbourg Grenadiers – killed, Lt Jones, 3 privates, wounded Capt. Cosnan, Lts Pinhorne, Nevin, 47 privates

Royal Train of Artillery – killed, 1 gunner, wounded, Lt Benzell, an engineer, 1 bombardier, 1 gunner, 5 matrosses.

List of French Prisoners – Capt. M. de Jourdeneau, Chev. De St Louis, of the regiment de Bearn; M. de Marisser, of de Languedoc; M. de Vours, of la Sarre, Lts. M. de Tozon, of Guienne; M de Castes of Languedoc; M. Lanbany, of la Sarre, prisoners 144.

Marines – Capt. M de la Combiere, Chev. De St Louis, Lt. M. Montarville, Cadet M. de Carville, Capt. of Guienne regiment M. Darling, Chev. De St Louis, M. Chambeau, M. Dartigue, M. de Grave, Capt. of Rousillon, M. St Blanhaire, 189 soldiers.

Letters and extracts from private letters from Quebec. Including –
one from James Calcroft dated Quebec 20 September 1759 stating
"the regiment of Lascelles, Kennedy's and Wolfe's grenadiers did
wonders – yet the Highlanders, if anything, exceeded them. When
these took to their broadswords what a havoc they made!. They
drove everything before them and the walls could not resist their fury.
Those breechless fellows are an honour to their country ....". From
an officer in Lascelles " Ewan Cameron, a common Highlander, killed
no less than 9 Frenchmen, among them two officers, when his sword
arm was cut off by a shot. He immediately snatched up a bayonet
and wounded several more, but an unlucky bullet penetrating his
throat, levelled him with the ground...". From an officer of Fraser's,
"the loss of our regiment is as follows. Captain Thomas Ross of
Culrossie, and Lt. Roderick McNeil of Barra, and Alexander
McDonnell, son to Barisdale, killed. Capt. S. Fraser of Inverallochy,
and John McDonald of Lochgarry, Lt. Macdonald of Keppoch,
Archibald Campbell, brother to Glenlyon, Alexander Campbell and
Douglas, and Ensigns Mackenzie, Malcolm Fraser, and gregorson
wounded. Colonel Fraser and Lt. Charles and Hector MacDonalds
and H. Cameron, were wounded but have recovered."

****

SOURCE: SM.21.557, [October 1759]

Died at the Siege of Quebec, of a flux, Alexander Cameron of
Dungallon

****

SOURCE: NAS.CC8.8

Confirmation of the testament of George Campbell, Lieutenant of the
Artillery, 26 October 1759 Commissariat of Edinburgh.

****

SOURCE: NAS.CS16.1.105, pp.238/292

Captain John McVicar, late of Lord John Murray's Highlanders v.
Colin Campbell of Ardualious, 24 November 1759

****

SOURCE: SM.21.593, [November 1759]

Extract from a private letter dated Quebec 10 October describing the
situation there. An extract from a letter dated Charleston, South
Carolina, 3 October 1759 with a report from Forts Loudoun and
George, stating that the Cherokees had cut the lines of
communication and that 2 soldiers had been scalped. A letter from
Saludy reporting that settlers on the frontier had taken refuge in forts
to escape the Cherokee attacks.

****

SOURCE: SM.21.606, [November 1759]

Died at Quebec on 15 October 1759 from wounds received in the
battle of 13 September, Captain Simon Fraser, of Fraser's Regiment,
second son of Charles Fraser of Inverallochy.

****

SOURCE SM.22.50, [January 1760]

November 1759, died at Oswego, Lieutenant Colonel William
Farquhar of Abercrombie's Foot.

****

SOURCE: SM.21.654, [December 1759]

An account of General Amherst's proceedings

****

SOURCE: SM.22.38, [January, 1760]

Report on conflict with the Cherokee Indians and an attack on Mr Atkins, the Indian agent and superintendent of trade with the southern Indians at a conference held with the Creeks on 28 September in Tuckabatches town. Captain Demere, commander of Fort Loudon, and Captain Stuart, commander of Fort Prince George, had advised that the Cherokee were on the warpath. Advice from Georgia confirmed that he Cherokees were attacking settlers in the back country. The son of Malatchi, a warrior and old friend of the British, with other friendly chiefs had come to Savannah to talk with Governor Ellis on 9 October. The Governor had brought in soldiers to protect the town and had sent Captain Milledge with his rangers to join the militia at Augusta. The Cherokee and the British had agreed to mutual peace and to fight against the French and their allies.

****

SOURCE: NAS.RH2/4/561/19.

Report of action in Carolina against the Cherokees in 1760, referring to Major Monipenny; the death of Ensign Munro and 10 men of the 22 and the Ensign Knight of the Royals, Lieutenant Barber and Ensign Campbell of Burtons, plus Lieutenant Terry of the Provincials and 10 men were wounded.

****

SOURCE: NAS.CS16.1.105, P352

Decreet, John Campbell of Kilpunt, v. Christian Murray, spouse to Lieutenant John Campbell of the Royal Highland Regiment, 9 January 1760.

****

SOURCE: NAS.CS16.1.106, p.354

Decreet, Helen Gibson, spouse to Francis Russel, surgeon general
to the army in America, 26 January 1760.

****

SOURCE: NAS.RH.2/4/561/20

A letter from Jeffrey Amherst in New York dated 24 February 1760 to
Colonel Montgomery advising him that a battalion of the Royals
under Major Hamilton and a battalion of Montgomery's Highlanders
under Major Grant were being sent to support him in his action
against the Cherokee Indians.

****

SOURCE: SM.22.51, [January, 1760]

In the neighborhood of Glasgow, Captain Alexander Campbell of
Inverawe, of the Argyllshire regiment. He was wounded in 1758 at
the attack upon Ticonderoga and never recovered from his wounds.
The attack occasioned also the death of his father who was Major of
the Royal Highland Regiment.

****

SOURCE: SM.22.154, [March, 1760]

Report that on 13 September Major Rogers marched from Crown
Point with 200 men and on 3 October they came within sight of the
Indian town St Francois, by which time his men now numbered 142.
At daybreak they attacked the town and killed between 200 and 300
there. From Charleston, South Carolina, came a report that the
Cherokee had broken their peace treaty with the British. They had

unsuccessfully attempted to enter Fort Prince George due to the vigilance of Lieutenant Coytmore, and thereafter had attacked traders and the settlements of Long Cane and the Forks of Broad River. The Georgia Rangers had been ordered to Augusta, Lieutenant Shaw and Ensign Macintosh had marched independent companies to reinforce Forts Moore and Augusta, and to relieve Lieutenant Outerbridge there.

****

SOURCE: NAS.RH1.2.776

Letter from Alexander Farquharson on an expedition against Fort Levi, Isle Royal, North America, 1760.

****

SOURCE: SM.22.211, [April 1760]

Accounts of the Cherokee Indian war received from Charleston dated 16 February 1760. Despatches had been brought to Charleston from Captain Paul Demere at Fort Loudon by Abraham, a Negro slave of Samuel Behan a trader, who had been given his freedom as a reward – there was a garrison of 180 men in the fort – the Upper Nation was quiet, except Settiquo from where war parties had set out for Virginia – Old Hop of Chote was dead – the Little Carpenter and Great Warrior of Chote 'still possessed much friedship for the English' – Mr Goudie's house had been burnt down – Samuel Behn was slightly wounded – Andrew Williamson had been shot through the sleeve but was unhurt - Mr Davis when escorting 23 women and children was attacked by the Indians near Steven's creek – Macartan and Campbell had built a stockade a mile from Fort Augusta – John Tobler had erected another near Fort Moore, as had Mr Galphin, also Rae and McGillivray – at James Germany's, twelve miles from Broad River, 600 people were building defences. From Fort Prince George came an account of the Indians attempting to seize the fort and mentioning the actions of Mr Dogharty, Lieutenant

Coylmore, Ensign Bell and Foster the interpreter. A party of 250 settlers moving from Long Canes to Augusta, Georgia, had been attacked by the Cherokees and 50 of them killed including Patrick Colquhoun. A letter from New York dated 10 March 1760 said that 600 of the Royal Scots and 600 of Montgomery's Highlanders were embarking for South Carolina to resist the Cherokees.

****

SOURCE: NAS.CC8.8

Confirmation of the testament of John Fallow, a soldier of Captain Robinson's Company of Highlanders, 10 September 1760, Commissariat of Edinburgh.

****

SOURCE: NAS.NRAS#0061/18

Letters from Alexander Farquharson from Fort Ontario, Montreal, Staten Island, Albany, and elsewhere in America describing his military experiences, 1760-1762.

****

SOURCE: SM.22.322, [June 1760]

A letter from Hon. James Murray, Governor of Quebec, to William Pitt dated 25 May 1760 reporting on military operations in the vicinity of Quebec on 28 April 1760 with a return of the killed and wounded –

AMHERST'S REGIMENT, killed - Lt. Maxwell sr., 4 sergeants, 21 privates, wounded – Capt.Lt. Cockburn, Lts. Mukins, Maxwell jr., Cathcart, Winter, Irving, and Lockhart, Ensigns Monepenny, Barbutt, Mills and Barker, 9 sergeants, 82 privates, prisoners – Lt. Hamilton and Ensign Montgomery.

BRAGG'S REGIMENT, killed – 4 sergeants, 14 privates, wounded – Colonel Walch, Major Dalling, Capts. Spann and Mitchelson, Lt.Adj. Taffel, Lts. Brown and Phibbs, Ensigns Gilmore, Shepherd and Beal, 4 sergeants, 3 drummers, 100 privates.

OTWAY'S REGIMENT, killed 12 privates, wounded – Lt. Brown, Ens. Lysaght, 3 sergeants, 1 drummer, 43 privates, prisoner – Capt. Ince.

KENNEDY'S REGIMENT, killed 5 privates, wounded – Captain Skey, Lt. Clements, 16 privates, prisoners Capt. Maitland and Ensign Maw.

LASCELLES REGIMENT, killed – Major Hussey, 1 sergeant, 10 privates, wounded – Lts. Foster, Basset, Ewer, Stratford, Ensigns Ustrich and Handfield, 3 sergeants, 1 drummer, 43 privates, prisoners – Capt. Archbold, Lt. Shirrett.

WEBB'S REGIMENT, killed – Ensign Nicholson, 22 privates, wounded – Capt. Lts. James Cockburn and Barbutt, Lts. Waterhouse, Royce, Crowe and More, Ensigns Campbell and Johnson, 63 privates, prisoner – Lt. Davers.

ANSTRUTHER'S REGIMENT, killed – Ens. Conway, 1 sergeant, 7 privates, wounded – 3 sergeants, 45 privates.

MONCKTON'S REGIMENT, killed – 1 drummer, 1 private, wounded – Ensigns Snow, Steel and Donald McDonald, 9 privates.

LAWRENCE'S REGIMENT, killed – 1 sergeant, 9 privates, wounded – Capt. Faesch, Lts. Faesch, Campbell, Grant, Stephens, and Lewis Forbes, Ensigns Pinckney, Magee, Hill and Steward, 32 privates, prisoners – Col. Young and Captain Charteris, missing – Lt. Forbes.

FRASER'S HIGHLANDERS, killed – Capt. Donald MacDonnel, Lt. Cosmo Gordon, 3 sergeants, 1 drummer, 51 privates, wounded – Col. Fraser, Capts. John Campbell, Alexander Fraser, and Macleod, Lts. Archibald Campbell, Hector MacDonald, Donald MacBean, Alexander Fraser sr., John Nairn, Arthur Rose, Alexander Fraser jr., Simon Fraser jr., Malcolm Fraser and Donald McNeil, Ensigns Henry Munro, Robert Menzies, Charles Stewart, Duncan Cameron, William Robertson, and Capt. Lt. Charles MacDonnel, 10 sergeants, 119 privates, prisoners – Ensigns Alexander Gregorson and Malcolm Fraser, missing – Lt. Alexander Campbell.

ARTILLERY, wounded – Major Goodwin, 2nd Lts. Heathcott and Scott, Lt.Fireworker Davidson, 3 bombardiers, 1 gunner, 6 mattrosses, prisoner – Lt. Fireworker Cock.
CHIEF ENGINEER, wounded Major Mackellar
LIGHT INFANTRY, killed – 8 sergeants, 78 privates, wounded – 7 sergeants, 1 drummer, 124 privates.
RANGERS, killed – 2 privates, wounded - Capt. Hazzen, 9 privates, missing – 1 mattross.

Extract of a letter from Charleston, 3 May 1760 –

Report of Cherokees near Fort Ninety Six who had killed and scalped Captain Francis's boy and taken John Downing a prisoner. Captain Francis, commander at Fort Ninety Six, and Mr Miln had written to the Lieutenant Governor and to Col. Montgomery and Col. Richardson.

****

SOURCE: SM.22.373, [July 1760]

A letter from an officer of the Royal American regiment giving an account of the proceedings at Quebec, 24 May 1760

An account by James Grant at camp near Fort Prince George of the campaign against the Cherokees in South Carolina, dated 4 June 1760, mentioning Lts Marshall and Hamilton of the Royals being wounded.

****

SOURCE: SM.22.437, [August 1760]

A report that the fortifications of Louisbourg had largely been destroyed and that by June 28, 1800 of the garrison were en route for Quebec. Generals Amherst and Gage were marching for Montreal via Oswego, with troops from New York, Connecticut and New

Jersey besides 7 regiments of regulars. Colonel Haviland was marching with 3 regiments of regulars, 4 New York Independent Companies, and troops from Rhode Island, New Hampshire and Massachusetts via Crown Point. Sir William Johnson had with him hundreds of Indians. Major Rogers had burnt a town between St John's and Chamblis called St Teresa and taken 40 prisoners, later he had been attacked and Captain Johnston of the Rangers and Ensign Wood of General Monckton's had been killed.

From Charleston came a report dated 21 June on the Cherokee campaign. James Holmes and .... Lucas were attacked and wounded. Jerome Courtonne had passed through Creek towns – John Ross a trader, William Mitchell his packhorseman, and Tom a Negro, William Rae a trader and his packhorseman William Robinson, Lauchlan Macintosh and George Johnston traders and John Robert, William Franks, and George MacCulloch packhorsemen, also Richard Hughes had been killed. A report from Fort Prince George said that one of the Highlanders was missing – mentions David Webb, Lieutenant of Grinnan's Rangers – Anthony Simmons a provincial soldier although scalped had survived.

****

SOURCE: NAS.RH1.2.765

H. A. Farquharson of the 42nd Highlanders in Montreal on 16 September 1760.

****

SOURCE: SM.22.481, [September 1760]

A report by Maj. Gen. Jeffrey Amherst at Fort William Augustus to Mr William Pitt, 26 August 1760, on the campaign in Canada, followed by the Articles for the Surrender of Canada.

Return of the killed and wounded –

ROYALS, killed – Capt. Williams, 9 privates, wounded – Capt. Peter Gordon, Ensign Eddington, 1 sergeant, 32 privates.
HIGHLANDERS, killed – 2 sergeants, 6 privates, wounded – Capt. Sutherland, Lts. MacMartin and McKinnon, Mr Munro the surgeon's mate, 1 sergeant, 2 corporals, 1 drummer, 22 privates.
PROVINCIALS, killed Capt. Morrison, 2 privates, wounded - Lt. Tatnell, 7 privates
WAGGONERS, killed – 1 private, wounded – Capt. Farrel, 2 privates.

An account of the Cherokee War

****

SOURCE: EUL, Laing Charters #3210, 3291, box 87]

27 October 1760, Commission by King George III appointing Normand Lamont to be Captain of the 89th [Highlanders] Regiment of Foot commanded by Lieutenant Colonel Staats Long Morris.

****

SOURCE SM.22.593, [November 1760]

Reports of the Articles of Capitulation signed by Captain Paul Demere and the officers of Fort Loudon with Cunni Catogue and Oucanastote on 7 July 1760. The garrison thereafter marched out of the fort leaving it to the Cherokee. However the column was attacked by Indians and all the officers, except Captain Stuart, killed along with 25 soldiers, and the rest made prisoners.

****

SOURCE: SM.22.662, [December 1760]

Letters of Captain Stuart concerning events after the garrison left Fort Loudon on 9 August 1760, refers to the killing of Captain

Demere, Lt. Adamson, Ensigns Bogges and Wintle and others at the hands of the Indians.

****

SOURCE: SM.22.710, [Appendix, 1760]

Extract of a letter from an officer in North America, to his friend in Ayr, dated Camp at Montreal, September 18, 1760.

****

SOURCE: NAS.GD87/89

A letter to John Campbell of Barcaldine from his son Lieutenant Colonel Alexander Campbell advising him of his appointment as Lieutenant Colonel to Colonel Burton's regiment in South Carolina. New York, 30 April 1761.

****

SOURCE: NAS.GD248. 507/3]

Letter from Captain Robert Grant in New York about to set out on an expedition, 1761.

****

SOURCE: NAS.NRAS#0631/48

Letter from James Campbell at Fort Prince George, 310 miles north-west of Charles Town, 1761.

****

SOURCE NAS.GD126. box 29/12-13]

Commissions of General Robert Melville as colonel of foot in America only; and as brigadier general in America only, 1761.

****

SOURCE: NAS.GD103.2.412

Commission by Sir Jeffery Amherst, Commander in Chief of HM Forces in America to Lieutenant Alexander Shaw as adjutant of the 60th [Royal American] Regiment of Foot, 6 October 1761.

****

SOURCE: NAS.GD172/2529

Letter to Colonel James Robertson at New York from James Goldfrap seeking an ensigncy for his 13 year old son, 8 January 1762.

****

SOURCE: NAS.CC8.8

Confirmation of the testament of Captain Robert Murray of Lord John Murray's Highland Regiment, 4 February 1762 Commissariat of Edinburgh.

****

SOURCE: NAS.CC8.8.

Confirmation of the testament of Charles Edgar, Sergeant of the Royal Artillery, 23 February 1762, Commissariat of Edinburgh.

****

SOURCE: NAS.CC8.8.

Confirmation of the testament of John Campbell, Lieutenant of the 12th Regiment of Foot, 30 March 1762, Commissariat of Edinburgh.

****

SOURCE: NAS.CC8.8

Confirmation of the testament of William Duncan, Sergeant of the 4th Regiment of Foot at Guadaloupe, 25 August 1762, Commissariat of Edinburgh.

****

SOURCE: NAS.CC8.8

Confirmation of the testament of Lieutenant John Fraser, son of Alexander Fraser of Pitcalzean, 25 August 1762, Commissariat of Edinburgh.

****

SOURCE: NAS.GD21/486

Copy of an epitaph by Lieutenant Colonel Amherst for Roderick Mackenzie, Captain of the 77th Regiment, who was killed at the taking of Quide Vide, 13 September 1762, and a copy of the epitaph of Charles McDonald, Captain of the 78th Regiment, killed at the taking of Signet Hill, 15 September 1762, dated September 1762.

****

SOURCE: NAS.CC8.8

Confirmation of the testament of Charles Cockburn, Captain of the Royal Regiment of Foot, 27 November 1762, Commissariat of Edinburgh

****

SOURCE: NAS.GD21.487

Letter from John Peebles, possibly to Dr Charles Fleming, giving details of the recapture of St Johns by Lieutenant Colonel Amherst, dated 20 September 1762, St John's, Newfoundland.

****

SOURCE: AJ #771

A report concerning the capture of Newfoundland on 18 October 1762.

****

SOURCE: NAS.RH2.4.561.21

Return of troops embarked at Havanna for New York 30 November 1762

		Embarked	died on way	arrived in New York
Anne	Jersey Provincials	55	8	47
Elizabeth 2	22nd Regiment	16	2	14
	28th Regiment	10	-	10

Jane Elizabeth

	Connecticut Provls.	123	35	88
	Jersey Provls.	85	19	66
Young Samuel	Connecticut Provincials	12	-	12
Hopewell	New York Provincials	79	27	52
Nancy	Royal Regiment	2	-	2
	56th Regiment	11	-	11
Neptune	New York Provincials	85	23	62
	34th Regiment	16	3	13
Intrepid	New York Provincials	19	-	19
	Connecticut Provls.	79	4	75
Amity's Good Intent*	New York Provincials	89	29	60

*leaky, put into South Carolina where the men embarked on the Betsy which sailed from Charleston, S.C., but was wrecked on Long Island where 29 died at sea.

Patience   35th & 43rd
              Regiments   returned to Havanna where the
35th boarded the Betsy and Polly and the 43rd went on the sloop Patience.

****

SOURCE: NAS.CC8.

Lieutenant Lachlan Shaw, of Captain Paul Demeri's Independent Company in South Carolina, confirmation of testament 1 December 1762, Commissariat of Edinburgh

SOURCE: AJ #798

Edinburgh 18 April 1763 – "It is said that there are now only 6 of the original soldiers left, of Lord John Murray's Regiment, who sailed from Britain to America, at the beginning of the war."

****

SOURCE: NAS.GD21/488.

A letter from I. A. Dalyell, ADC to Major Lobel, commander of the 77th Regiment, informing him that the General had approved the application of John Peebles, surgeon's mate of the 77th Regiment, to be allowed to serve as a volunteer in that regiment, dated at New York 14 June 1763.

****

SOURCE: NAS.CS16.1.115, p.185

Captain John Gordon of one of the Independent Companies in New York, v. Alexander Gordon of Cairnfield and his eldest son John Gordon, 23 June 1763

****

SOURCE: NAS.RH2.4.561.23

List of troops under the command of Lieutenant Colonel Amherst, New York 13 August 1763

From New York 103 officers/men   under Captain Maxwell of
15th Regiment
88 officers/men under Captain Charles
McDonnell of the 78th Regiment

from Halifax 237 officers and men of the Royals
158 officers and men of Montgomery's
220 officer and men of the Massachusetts
Provincials
from Louisbourg 395 officers and men of the 45th Regiment
From New York 19 officers and men of the Royal Artillery
From Halifax 39 officers and men of the Royal Artillery

****

SOURCE: NAS.CC8.8.

Confirmation of the testament of Alexander Hutchison, Lieutenant
Colonel of Colonel Brigg's Regiment, 20 August 1761, Commissariat
of Edinburgh.

****

SOURCE: NAS.GD21/676

Commission by Major General Sir Jeffrey Amherst, Commander in
Chief of HM Forces in North America, in favor of John Peebles as
ensign in the 42nd Royal Highland Regiment, commanded by
Lieutenant General George Murray, 23 August 1763.

****

SOURCE: NAS.GD248.509/3.

Letter from Captain Robert Grant re a new Indian War, 1763.

****

SOURCE: NAS.GD87.1.95

Memo from the northern and Highland counties to the Secretary of War asking that the 77th [Montgomery's Highlanders] Regiment and the 78th [Fraser's Highlanders] be disbanded in Scotland, dated 1763.

****

SOURCE: NAS.GD172/2534

Receipts from Colonel Robertson of payment for transport of troops to Mobile, October 1763

****

SOURCE: NAS.GD172/2536

Accounts of gifts for the Choctaw and Creek Indians by Major Robert Farmer of the 34th Foot, Commander of Louisiana, October 1763.

****

SOURCE: NAS.GD172/2539

Receipt by Lieutenant Robert Lindsay from Colonel Robertson for expenses incurred when carrying despatches from Mobile to Pensacola, 15 December 1763.

****

SOURCE: NAS.NRAS#0631/51

Letters from James Campbell in New Orleans describing the country there and military affairs, including a voyage from New Orleans to Mobile, during which the boat was attacked by Indians, 1764.

****

SOURCE: NAS.RH4.22.1/2.

General account of fighting Indians after the peace treaty of 1763 and of expeditions to occupy the newly ceded territories, including a voyage of 100 men of the 42nd Regiment under Captain Thomas Stirling down the Ohio and Mississippi in 1765. A detailed account of a voyage of a detachment of the 42nd from Fort Pitt down the Ohio and up the Mississippi to occupy Fort Chartres in 1765.

****

SOURCE NAS.CS16.1.117, p.152

John Ross, writer in Edinburgh, V. Alexander Grant, late merchant, John Crichton, late merchant in Leith, John McDonald, soldier in Colonel Montgomery's Regiment, etc, 15 February 1764.

****

SOURCE: NAS.CC8.8.

Confirmation of the testament of Nicoll McGlashan, soldier of the 42nd Regiment of Foot commanded by Lord John Murray, 31 July 1764, Commissariat of Edinburgh.

****

SOURCE: NAS.RH15.176.8

William Haggart, a reduced subaltern officer of the 77th Regiment, granted land in Albany, New York, on the east side of Lake Champlain, 1765. [NAS.GD237, box 259, bundle 2; 237/21/21/1]

****

SOURCE: NAS.CC8.8.

Confirmation of the testament of John McNeill, Major of Lord John Murray's Regiment, 13 April 1765, Commissariat of Edinburgh.

****

SOURCE: NAS.CC8.8.

Confirmation of the testament of Archibald McNab, Lieutenant of the 42nd Regiment, 12 March 1766, Commissariat of Edinburgh.

****

SOURCE: NAS.CC8.8.

Confirmation of the testament of John Young, Colonel of the Royal American Regiment, 31 March 1766, Commissariat of Edinburgh.

****

SOURCE: NAS.CC8.8.

Confirmation of the testament of John Kennedy, soldier of Colonel Montgomery's Highlanders, 1 August 1767, Commissariat of Edinburgh.

****

REFERENCES

AJ	=	Aberdeen Journal, series
CA	=	Chronicles of Atholl & Tullibardine, [Edinburgh, 1908]
NAS	=	National Archives of Scotland
NLS	=	National Library of Scotland
SM	=	Scots Magazine, series

INDEX

Benzell, lt., 80
Bergabine, John, 51
Bevan, John, 47
Biggs, William, 47
Billings, Lt., 61
Bines, Robert, 43
Birchall, Ens., 22
Bird, Capt., 80
Bishop, Eneas, 7
Bisset, Ens, 63
Bizet, Donald, 13
Blair, John, 72
Blakeney, Lord, 46, 78
Blane, Archibald, 65
Bogges, Ens., 91
Boscawen, Adm., 36
Boston, 3, 16, 28, 50, 51, 52, 53
Bouquet, Henry, 42, 61
Bower, Andrew, 57
Boyd, Daniel, 44
Boyd, Robert, 31, 44
Boyle, Charles, 63
Braddock, General, 1, 33
Bradstreet,..., 38, 79
Braggs, Lt., 41
Breadalbane, Earl of, 8
Brechin, 11
Bredin, Capt., 40
Bremner, Alexander, 14,
Bremner, George, 23
Bremner, John, 12
Brewer, Peter, 52
Brigstock, Capt., 78
Broad River, 6, 85
Broadstreet, Col., 3, 5, 50
Broom,...,57
Brown, Charlotte, 31
Brown, Donald, 24
Brown, John, 56
Brown, Rowland, 50
Brown, Lt., 87

Cotter, Tim, 47
Cotteral, Thomas, 46
Cottnam, Lt., 54
Couce, William, 31
Courtonne, Jerome, 89
Coventry, Lt., 76
Cowie, William, 24
Cox, Capt., 54
Coytmore, Lt., 85, 86
Crafton, Ens., 40
Crawford, James, 45
Cree, David, 46
Crichton, John, 99
Criton, John, 45
Crofton, Lt., 37
Croton Camp, 42
Crowe, Lt., 87
Crown Point, 4, 5, 6, 7, 8, 32, 36, 37, 73, 74, 76, 84
Cruickshank, Capt., 50
Culbert, Lt., 30
Cumberford, Lt., 41
Cuming, James, 14
Cumming, Alexander, 62
Cumming, John, 62
Cunni Catogue, 90
Cunningham, Hugh, 44
Cunningham, Col., 75
Cuthbert, Donald, 13
Cuthbert, John, 33
Cuthbertson, James, 43
Dagworthy, John, 40, 63
Dainty, Ens., 80
Dalling, Maj., 87
Dalyell, I. A., 96
Danks, Capt., 79
Darby, John, 21
Darling, M., 80
Dartique, M., 80
Davers, Lt., 87
Davidson, Edward, 14
Davidson, George, 15

Hair, Lt., 37
Haldimand, Col., 29
Halifax, 18, 20, 25, 27, 43, 55, 56, 59, 97
Halket, Maj., 43
Haller, Ens., 61
Halls, James, 49
Hambight, Capt., 68
Hamilton, Alexander, 29
Hamilton, Archibald, 20
Hamilton, Frederick, 19
Hamilton, Gavin, 29
Hamilton, John, 29
Hamilton, Thoms, 44
Hamilton, William, 39
Hamilton, ..., 39, 70, 78, 79, 84, 86, 88
Hammond, Henry, 28
Handfield, Ens., 87
Handler, Ens., 67
Hanly, Cornet, 57
Hanyman, John, 48
Hapson, Gen., 51
Harris,....,64
Harrison, Aaron, 46
Harrison, Ens., 22, 64
Hars,...,57
Hart, Lt., 39
Harvey, Roger, 44
Harvey, Capt., 70
Haselwood, Lt., 41
Hassel, John, 44
Haviland, Cornelius, 44
Haviland, Col., 89
Hay, Alexander, 19
Hay, Lord Charles, 17, 23, 25,
Hay, Capt.,70
Hayes, Lt., 78
Hays, ..., 56, 64
Hazzen, Capt., 88
Healy, Patrick, 53
Heathcote, Lt., 88
Hellins, James, 47

115.

119

McLeod, Norman, 63
McLeod, Roderick, 25, 27
McLeod, Capt., 87
McLinnion, William, 63
McManus, James, 19
McMartin, Lt., 90
McMillan, Neil, 3
McMullen, James, 48
McMullen, Mary, 48
McMullen, Neal, 44
McMyne, William, 31
McNab, Archibald, 100
McNab, James, 62
McNab, Thomas, 24
McNeil, Andrew, 44
McNeil, Donald, 63, 87
McNeill, John, 100
McNeill, Neill,12, 63
McNeil, Roderick, 81
McNeil, Rory, 9, 80
McNeil, William, 51
McNeill, Capt., 55
McNicol, Duncan, 67, 77
McOwan, Alexander, 47
McPhail, John,10, 17
McPhee, Hugh, 63
McPhee, John, 63
McPherson, Alexander, 24, 63
McPherson, Colin, 46
McPherson, Donald, 15, 43
McPherson, Hugh, 38, 40
McPherson, James, 24, 72
McPherson, Kenneth,15
McPherson, Malcolm, 43, 59
McPherson, Robert, 44
McPherson, William, 33
McQueen, Donald, 63
McQueen, John, 24
McRaw, Donald, 24
McVicar, John, 82
Magee, Ens., 87

Maginnis, Capt., 21
Mahoney,....,57
Maitland, Capt., 78, 87
Malatchi, 83
Malloy, John, 27
Marlow, Richard, 51
Marsh, Capt., 40
Marshall, Lt., 88
Martin, Ens., 21
Martingall, William, 9
Mason, William, 80
Mather, Richard, 41, 58
Mathison, Lt., 78
Matthew, Lt., 64
Maturin, Gabriel, 80
Maunsell, Capt., 49
Maw, Ens., 87
Maxwell, John, 79
Maxwell, Lt., 86
Maxwell, Capt., 96
Mearns, 11
Meech, Lt., 79
Melville, Robert, 91
Menzies, Alexander, 23, 66
Menzies, Charles, 62
Menzies, Duncan, 46
Menzies, Robert, 24, 34, 87
Mercer, James, 24
Mercer, Colonel, 3, 6
Meredith, Samuel, 59, 60
Michall, James, 63
Miles, Lt., 67
Mill, Alexander, 47
Mill, David, 40, 62
Millbank, Acomb, 79
Milledge, Capt., 83
Miller, Matthew, 13
Mills, Ens., 86
Miln, ..., 88
Milne, James, 69
Mirrie, Robert, 19

Bragg's, 16, 20, 35, 38, 39, 78, 79, 86, 97
Burton's, 83
Cambise, 38
Cameronian, 1
Connecticut, 95
De Bearn, 80
Delancey's, 41
De Languedoc, 80
Demeri's, 7
Engineers, 53, 75, 79
Ferrill's, 7
Fitch's, 41
Forbes's, 16, 20, 21, 32, 36, 38, 39, 42, 44, 45, 57,
Fraser's, 10, 12, 18, 28, 30, 36, 37, 38, 39, 42, 75, 77, 79, 80, 82, 86,
      98
Gage's, 36, 41
Guienne, 80
Grenadier's, 19, 26, 30, 79, 80, 81
Guyenne, 6
Hopson's, 20, 36
Howe's, 36, 40, 41
Johnston's, 41
Keith's, 77
Kennedy's, 16, 20, 78, 80, 81, 86
La Sarre, 80
Lascelles's, 20, 36, 70, 78, 80, 81, 86
Laurence's, 79, 80, 86
Loudon's, 1, 2,16
Marines, 17, 39, 79
Massachusetts, 97
Maryland, 59, 61, 63, 64, 70
Monckton's, 38, 39, 78, 80, 86
Montgomery's, 8, 10, 18, 30, 36, 65, 84, 86, 90, 97, 98, 99, 100
Murray's, 2, 4,16, 20, 36, 37, 40, 45, 60, 70, 77, 82, 90, 96, 100
New Jersey, 21, 25, 94, 95
New York, 21, 25, 95
North Carolina, 61 ,64
Otway's, 25, 36, 38, 39, 70, 78, 80, 86
Partridge's, 41
Pennsylvania, 61, 64, 67, 69
Pepperall's, 6

Perry's, 17, 20, 45
Prebble's, 41
Rangers, 20, 36, 37, 38, 39, 79, 85, 88, 89
Royal Americans,1, 7, 16, 20, 21, 27, 29, 36, 41, 48, 50, 58, 61, 64, 69,
    71, 88, 91,100
Royal Artillery, 20, 40, 79, 80, 81, 88, 91, 97
Royal Scots, 16, 20, 36, 37, 38, 54, 66, 70, 83, 84, 86, 88, 90, 94, 95,
    97
Rousillon, 80
Sarre, 6
Schuyler's, 6
Shirley's, 6
Virginia, 54, 58, 60, 61, 63, 64, 72
Volontaires Estangers, 39
Warburton's, 20, 36, 71
Webb's, 20, 36, 38, 39, 50, 71, 78, 80, 86
Whitmore's, 20, 36, 38, 39, 44,
Worster's, 41
3rd, 33
4th, 93
12th, 93
15th, 96
17th, 21, 29, 33, 45, 69, 71
22nd, 46, 54, 57, 83, 94
27th, 46
28th, 94
34th, 95, 98
35th, 51, 95
40th, 51, 52, 54, 69
42nd, 2, 4, 5, 9, 23, 24, 37, 38, 45, 46, 60, 62, 99, 100
43rd, 95
44th, 6, 26, 47
45th, 26, 28, 50, 54, 97
46th, 47
47th, 52, 54
48th, 24, 27, 47
50th, 32
55th, 18, 41
56th, 95
60th, 1, 16, 29, 42, 65, 91
63rd, 10, 28, 33